GLENN GOES GLOBAL

TALES OF A FOOTLOOSE COLONIAL

GLENN FOWLER

First published in Australia in 2004 by
New Holland Publishers (Australia) Pty Ltd
Sydney • Auckland • London • Cape Town

14 Aquatic Drive Frenchs Forest NSW 2086 Australia
218 Lake Road Northcote Auckland New Zealand
86 Edgware Road London W2 2EA United Kingdom
80 McKenzie Street Cape Town 8001 South Africa

10 9 8 7 6 5 4 3 2 1

National Library of Australia Cataloguing-in-Publication Data:

Fowler, Glenn, 1972–.
Glenn goes global: tales of a footloose colonial.

ISBN 1 74110 096 8

1. Fowler, Glenn, 1972—Journeys. 2. Voyages and travels.
3. Teachers, Foreign—Great Britain. 4. Europe—Description
and travel. 5. Great Britain—Description and travel. I. Title.

910.4

Publishing Manager: Robynne Millward
Senior Editor: Monica Ban
Designer: Karlman Roper
Printer: Griffin Press, Adelaide

This book was typeset in Aldine 10.5pt

Contact Glenn at glennfowler1972@yahoo.co.uk

Contents

Prologue

During my recent travels, I learned an awful lot about people. As a history graduate and high school teacher, I reckon I've got two pretty good reasons to view the human race with some pessimism. As the former, I've spent years grappling with the appalling vices of man. (I've long believed that references to despicable humans as 'animals' are grossly unfair to animals, that generally kill out of instinct and need. Humans are, I believe, capable of the best, but also the worst possible behaviour.) And as the latter, having spent more than eight years in the government education system, I've seen enough apathy, selfishness and disrespect to last me a lifetime. This is not to say that I've lost all faith. I've certainly never seriously entertained taking up the life of a hermit. On the contrary, I've lived a hugely social life and have always surrounded myself with friends from all walks of life. Still, when I decided to take up a one year teaching position in England in August 2001, I thought my greatest memories would be of the exotic locations I visited during the school holidays. Little did I know how close I would become to a new batch of friends and how many laughs I would share. The people I met form the fondest and most enduring memories of my year away. In this collection of stories, I'd like to tell you about some of them.

Glenn Fowler
Canberra
February 2004

For Marina—my favourite person of all—
and the reason for my return.

Acknowledgements

This book would not have materialised without the assistance of others.

I'll start by acknowledging all those who read my cathartic emails from abroad and suggested I have a go at a book. I honestly don't believe I would have thought of it otherwise.

I would like to thank all of my friends who permitted me to include their names, stories and photographs in the book, and who jogged my memory when I needed it.

I am indebted to my team of pre-submission proofreaders—Alex and Kath, Anna, Fi and Nicky. Boxes of chockies and tubes of Apricot Body Dew will never be recompense enough.

A million thanks go to Clare Moss, without whom the road to publication would undoubtedly have been a longer one. Forever snowed under with professional editing jobs, Clare made time for me constantly—advising, editing, encouraging. I'll never forget the help she provided.

I have always dreamed of being a rock star, but getting published as a writer is an unexpected delight. For this near miracle, I am grateful to Robynne, Monica and the rest of the team at New Holland. You guys have made my year.

I am grateful to my father Trevor who, in his inimitable way, provided practical help as always. The only catch is that now, for the first time in forty years, he'll have to read a book. He'd damn well better!

My particular thanks go to my mother Robyn, who helped to proofread the manuscript and always said the right things. I know she'll be proud of me.

And to the beautiful Marina: thanks for letting me go, thanks for taking me back, thanks for letting me spend days at a time on your computer, thanks for putting up with my computer rage, thanks for listening to me read each new chapter and laugh at my own jokes, and thanks for being as excited as I was when it all came off. Thank you for being you, Fin.

One
Stevenage: Educating Ritalin

I blame Hitler for Stevenage. Had the bastard not ordered the bombing of London's suburbs during World War II, there would have been no post-war housing shortage and, hence, no need to create 'new towns' like Stevenage in Hertfordshire.

Stevenage was actually a Roman town before becoming a popular stopover for northbound medieval travellers on their first night out of the capital. Many of the inns and coach houses still remain. After the Blitz, Stevenage's 'Old Town' was enveloped by a network of dull and uninspiring estates, along with a shopping district that makes communist-era Eastern Europe look like the work of Barcelona's Gaudi. Coming from Canberra, Australia's modern, carefully planned and (if you listen to the critics), 'artificially neat' capital, I could at least appreciate the feeling of spaciousness created by the boulevards, roundabouts and parklands in various parts of Stevenage. Both places, due to the era of their constructions, had been designed for the automobile. I must admit, though, that these observations were usually made on particularly homesick days. Roundabouts aside, the two places are miles apart in terms of landscaping, architectural design and style. Stevenage's only real saving grace is that it doesn't take long to escape to one of several surrounding villages, all of which are classically English and contain a good country pub. For those of us forced to re-enter Stevenage, this was a frequent but all too brief respite.

Stevenage is home to around 75 000 people and seems to be growing. Many of its inhabitants are employed in public administration (local government, hospitals, schools), and many others work in the manufacturing and service industries. The people of Stevenage are by no means deprived in economic terms but, as

I was told early on in my stay, many are 'academically deprived' and 'culturally poor'. I often had cause to wonder just how many books there were in the homes.

Stevenage is a truly provincial place. Colleagues and friends of mine would joke that there is in fact an invisible wall around the town preventing anyone from getting out. (I wish it had prevented me from getting in!) Indeed, the twenty-five-minute train journey to London—one of the world's liveliest cities—is almost never made by most Stevenage people I met. I've done a fair bit of travelling in my time, including Third World areas in Asia, Africa and South America, and I've experienced plenty of culture shocks. It seems grossly naive of me in hindsight, but I honestly thought that people in a predominantly non-industrial, urban environment in the south of England would not be all that dissimilar in experience and attitude to myself. I did not expect much of a culture shock at all, let alone one of this enormity.

I went to England partially to absorb a different culture and to live a different day-to-day existence. My main objective, though, was to travel again. I wanted to see the 'fringes' of Europe that I had missed during a three-month jaunt with my girlfriend in 1997—Ireland, Portugal, Scandinavia, Hungary, Poland (which, alas, I missed again) and wherever else tickled my fancy. To do this I needed money. At the age of twenty-nine, I was ineligible for a 'working visa', a document that would see me working in a job of my choosing for as long as it suited me. An 'ancestry visa' was also out of the question on account of the fact that my parents had not had the decency to ensure that at least one of their parents was British. My 'work permit' was, in effect, an entry to the country sponsored by an employer. My skills are in high school teaching. I have the ability to persuade, trick, cajole, threaten and bully increasingly unmotivated and (usually quite contentedly) alienated post-pubescents to shut the hell up and at least pretend to learn. As it happened, Stevenage's Slothwick Skool (my spelling) was looking for precisely these skills.

'Stevenage?' I responded to my recruitment agent over the telephone. 'Is it near London?'

'Thirty minutes by train,' came the reply.

'Is it alright?' I asked, sceptical of the rather bizarre name. To me it sounded like Darrenage or Jasonage.

'Yes, it's alright. Quite nice really.'

'Let me look it up on the Net.'

Isn't it amazing how websites can turn dog turd into crème caramel? With its 'rich and varied history' (a few inns now selling real estate or vindaloos), its 'charming pubs' (where a shaved head seems to be a prerequisite), and its 'lively nightclubs' (with the average age either sixteen or forty-six depending on whether you frequented Pulse or Vogue), this town sounded pretty good. Besides, I wanted to be close to London but not in it (on account of the cost of living), so this seemed perfect. Fortunately, as I was about to leave Australia, my soon-to-be boss told me that I might consider living outside of Stevenage, as somewhere like nearby Hitchin might be 'more appropriate for the young professional'. Now that I know Vaughan well, I know that he was really saying: 'Whatever you do, don't live in that shit hole.' It was the best piece of advice I received all year. Thank God I followed it.

So, after my initial research, Stevenage seemed okay. But what about the school? A friend of mine told me that I should check out Slothwick Skool's OFSTED report (The Office of Standards in Education), available on the Internet. OFSTED inspects all British Government schools on a five or six year rotation. The reports are very detailed and I encourage any antipodeans intending to take advantage of the chronic teacher shortage in the UK (which has hit about five years before Australia's will) to see what sort of rating their prospective school achieved. Mine did pretty well when it was last inspected in December 1996. My mistake was to assume that not much could have changed in the intervening five year period. What I didn't know was that in 1997 the school had changed head teachers (principals). Anyone who has worked in a school will tell you that an ineffective head can kill it. I've known of it happening in Canberra, and in 2001, it was happening at Slothwick. The school was about to have its next OFSTED inspection as I departed and the word was that the only thing that would save it from being placed on 'special measures' (one step above a failure) was its proximity to Slagmore School. At Slagmore, from several accounts, a teacher judged their day by how much spit they had to wash out of their hair. They couldn't have two schools in the area going down.

Having accepted the position and packed my bags, it wasn't long before I was in the classroom. I had ten classes—a load that would make any Aussie teacher shudder. One thing that struck me immediately was the mono-cultural nature of the student population. Coming from multicultural Canberra, I was used to having more than a sprinkling of Mohammeds, Ching-Yis and Toshikis in my classes. Of the two hundred and sixty children I taught in Stevenage, I estimate that two hundred and fifty-five were from Anglo-Celtic stock. These kids knew very little about the world and I was starting to understand why. They had very little exposure to anything or anyone different.

It was soon clear that I was not only from a different country, but a different planet from my little protégés. I've known my fair share of lazy and naughty students in Canberra, but there are generally a few inquisitive, worldly, relatively informed whipper-snappers to provide a modicum of intellectual stimulation. I swear to you, I was not stimulated in this or any other fashion during my eleven months at Slothwick. These were children who, at the age of fifteen, could not (as a class) come up with explanations for terms like colony, democracy, monarchy or republic. They could however, to a person, list the six new signings for football (soccer) club West Ham United and, if pushed, provide their mothers' maiden names. The first president of the United States, the inventor of the telephone, the author of *Hamlet*, the artist who painted the *Mona Lisa*...not a hope. But if you ever needed to know the name of the assistant manager of Tottenham Hotspur, these were your people.

Seeing each of my ten classes for only four hours a fortnight would, you might think, make learning their names a problem. Not really. (If in doubt, Lauren, Sarah, Ben or Richard were all pretty safe bets.) The problem was that they seemed to forget who I was. Retraining occurred at the beginning of each lesson.

That's right, kiddies. I'm not your RE (Religious Education) teacher. I expect you to walk, not dive, into the room. I'm going to give you some work, I expect you to attempt it, I will not be called a 'prick', and I strongly object to being punched on the chin.

They'd get it eventually, but not before asking approximately one billion moronic questions...

'Which side of the ruler do I use?'

'What book are we using?'

'What day is it?'

'Where am I?'

These were the most utterly dependent people I'd ever met, typified by an interesting phenomenon which I've termed 'desk creep'. Every week, I would need to spend five minutes pulling each student desk towards the back of the room (and further away from me). It was like *The Day of the Triffids*, only instead of plants coming to get me, it was desks. Subconsciously, it seems, these kids needed to be all over me, demanding 'the answer' and requiring repetition of relevant page numbers (even if I'd written them on the board) to a comical degree. Everywhere I turned, they were upon me—in the hallways, in the car park, on the way home. The staffroom was like a bunker, and in it I sought refuge. These children were, in every sense of the term, 'high maintenance'.

Assisting Year 8 students in spelling their names correctly was the sort of task I never expected to perform. Had Laura spelt her name without the 'h' on the end, I might have been tempted to award her a mark on her test. She certainly could have done with it. A Year 9 girl recorded her homework in her diary: 'Lean spellings'. When looking at ideas surrounding heaven and hell in the medieval church, the concept of purgatory is usually raised. Why the nation of Paraguay rated such a continuous mention in this exercise was a mystery to me, until I realised that it was probably the suggestion of the PC's spellcheck.[1]

Slothwick kids don't really do humour, unless of course it involves spitting, hurling projectiles or wiping dog shit on each other. Even *they* found the following incident funny. One day I was sitting at my desk at the front of the room. I told my Year 7 class to open their workbooks and (I said, while pointing at the whiteboard), 'write the title behind me'. Five minutes later whilst doing my rounds, I noticed that everyone had written the title 'What is slavery?', except one boy. His title was 'Behind Me'.

Buoyed by their laughter, I thought perhaps I could revert to my previous teaching style—stand-up comedy. It had worked at home after all. One day I was trying to teach the notorious 8Cc, named after their form tutor Mr Cochise. I always wondered why they hadn't stuck to the formula and called the class 8Co. Then I saw the genius of the Deputy Principal. In two years time they would be 10Cc, in honour of the 1970s band who generously gave us songs like 'The Things We Do For Love'. After a lesson with these nutcases, it was clear to me that Mr Cochise wasn't 'doing it for love'. Like me, he was strictly in it for the

---

[1] I would like to say that one positive of my teaching year was watching those few kids who were prepared to listen improve in leaps and bounds. I've never seen such rapid improvement, and I'd like to think it was helped along by the introduction of a bit of rigour and the fairly high standards to which I stubbornly adhered.

cash. Anyway, one day an 8Cc-ite farted in class. You'd probably recognise the standard teacher response to an occurrence of this nature: 'You dirty boy—don't do it again!' or 'Go outside until you've learnt some bowel control!' On this particular day, I thought I'd try a new tack, inspired by *Caddyshack*'s Rodney Dangerfield. 'Somebody step on a duck?!' I exclaimed, inwardly amused by my lack of maturity, but outwardly deadpan. Now at home I'd get a few laughs for this outburst, but in Stevenage, I got twenty-five looks of 'What are you talking about?' and one muppet looking around and asking: 'What duck?' Of course, the inevitable next fart, on which I was too deflated to comment, received far more laughter.

Farts really are big at Slothwick. The boys generally crank them out and, believe it or not, the girls seem to dig it. Not as much as they dug the sight of me stumbling out of the classroom in search of oxygen. All that white bread…and those sausages…

Personal hygiene was not exactly the strongpoint of many of my students. One day a Year 7 girl presented herself at my desk, thrusting her hand in my face. 'I went to the doctor,' she said, 'and he says I've got scabies…look! My whole family's got 'em!' 'Fantastic!' I thought. At least when I was teaching about life in Victorian slums, I could use her as a visual aid. Another day a boy approached me mumbling something about 'toiley'.

'Sorry,' I said, 'I don't speak gibberish.'

'Mr Fowler,' he said, his face rapidly turning red, 'I need to go poo.' This boy was in Year 9. On one occasion, we took the same boy on a school trip. His mother, in a letter addressed 'To whom it *make* concern' (How right she was!), explained that if he didn't take his pills at 7.30 a.m., 1.00 p.m., 5.00 p.m. and 9.00 p.m. then 'that mean trouble'. We didn't need to know exactly what 'trouble' we were in for—we just dealt the drugs.

Some children acted strangely for medical reasons. Others were loonies, pure and simple.

Denis was an occasionally likeable (but more often infuriating) rogue in my Year 10 class. He took a keen interest in my Australianness and, unlike most of his peers, could point to my homeland on a map. (Others asked me if I was going home for Christmas lunch, while some senior students asked me when Christmas occurred Down Under…and I did get tired of explaining that I didn't personally know Steve Irwin, The Crocodile Hunter.) Denis lost some credibility with me, however, when he fell victim to the same temptation as many of the others—the temptation to say 'G'day mate' (Hoges style) to me every day for eleven months without showing any sign of getting sick of it. Denis's major problem, though, was his inability to control his mouth. He persistently blurted out things in a public forum that landed him in varying degrees of strife. It can be quite off-putting when teaching a senior history class to hear a cry of 'Beef curtains!', or the slightly more refined 'Sausage jockey!' At other times he would, without warning, claim to 'need some love juice' or invite nobody in particular to 'lick his furry ring piece!' Adaptability was his gift. Any discussion of Australia would inevitably warrant a call of 'Aborigine!', or that old chestnut 'G'day!' When discussing cowboys in the American West, 'Mooooo!' was often a good one. I discovered that he could deliver this with real versatility of both volume and pitch, and I even started to use him strategically as a sort of soundtrack to the lesson. Each time I read the word 'cow' or 'cowboy' I would pause and, on cue and without fail, there was my 'Moooo!' It was more challenging for him to work in a blood-curdling, chicken-like 'Begork!!!', but he managed it. After two months of, in turn, chastising him, jollying him along and asking him if he'd heard of 'Tourette's', I was informed that his mother had actually made inquiries about the syndrome. I'm comfortable in the knowledge that Tourette's sufferers don't exactly give thought to selecting bizarre terms with maximum shock value. Denis was quite capable of toning it down (and turning it off for that matter). He showed enough respect for the staff and worshippers at historic St Albans Cathedral to mention only 'Beef!' or 'Sausages!'

School trips were always a treat. My first experience was taking a bus-full of ghetto-pimp-wannabes to the big smoke (London) to see a theatrical production. Their attire—three-quarter length navy blue track pants, hooded navy blue sweatshirt and navy blue denim jacket—along with their cocky banter on the bus, had me worried that they were going to 'express themselves'. My colleagues gave them an hour's free time prior to the show during which they could roam the streets of London. At the appointed meeting time and place, I half-expected those that turned up to be sporting a few 'hot' stereos or even 'motors'. What I saw was a herd of deer caught in the headlights, who had made it as far as McDonalds, become scared by traffic, noise and people who looked 'funny', and returned ten minutes early. They were there waiting for us! Apparently on a previous trip some of them had been approached by a group of toughs who had asked one of them, 'How much money you got?' The Slothwick boy cleverly replied, 'Twenty-five pounds'. The toughies said, 'Give it 'ere' and the boy said, 'Okay'. He later demanded that one of the teachers give chase.

A lovable little anecdote emerged from our Year 10 daytrip to the Galleries of Justice in Nottingham. Here, in an early nineteenth century prison, kids wander through preserved and reconstructed courtrooms and cells, reliving the harshness of prison life in pre-Victorian and Victorian times. Their experience is enhanced by a troupe of actors who (undoubtedly having the time of their lives), push, shove, scream at and bully the students into oblivion. At one point, after making us walk clockwise around a tiny courtyard for ten minutes, a gaoler turned to a tall, well-proportioned, attractive girl with long blonde hair and bellowed:

'You've got something I could really use in here! Do you know what that might be?'

The girl, Nelly, sheepishly replied, 'Yes.'

'Well?!' he persisted.

'My body,' mumbled Nelly.

Somewhat bemused, the gaoler bellowed, 'NO! Your hair!'

On three separate days, we took a large group of Year 8 students to Ye Olde Stevenage, a five-minute bus ride from the school. The Old Town consists of a high street with a selection of medieval buildings interspersed with newer, less appealing constructions. If you know where to look, there are certainly some points of historical interest (coach houses, stables, stairs and walls designed to accommodate the transport of the day), and the idea was to show them where to look. On the first day, a lad told us that his mother had 'been there as a girl', like it was the Royal Albert Hall or something…

…It was 1974. I can remember the day as if it were yesterday. The sun was shining, the birds were chirping. We had a pitcher of lemonade and the bus driver let us listen to the wireless… suddenly there it was…Stevenage Old Town!

On the second day, members of the public on two separate occasions told our little darlings (one of whom had stuck her head into the front window of a pub and tried to sip from a pint) to 'Fuck off!' We stopped at one point for them to sketch a row of medieval almshouses. These had been built to house the poor several hundred years ago and today, it seems, have become private residences. I told the students to note the medieval TV aerials. Head of Department, Vaughan—a short, energetic Welshman in his mid-thirties with a sharp wit and healthy degree of cynicism—delivered the sad news that the antiquity of these aerials meant that the occupants could only pick up episodes of *The Flintstones* and *Blackadder*. They bought every word.

On the third and final day of this exercise, we saw a coffin that had been lodged in the rafters of a barn for three hundred years, originally at the request of the occupant in order to foil opportunistic body snatchers looking to make a pound or two from medical researchers. Most students, to their credit, had been looking forward to this all day and were genuinely interested in what they saw and the story associated with it. You'll have noticed I said *most* students. Laurette Scrimmins, being the most repulsive individual I have ever had the misfortune of teaching (and that's no mean feat) deserves a couple of lines at this point. Laurette Scrimmins is the type of person whose first thought on waking each morning is: 'Right, who can I piss off today?' I would hear her coming from one hundred metres away, bounding along clumsily, using her bulk to injure people and damaging their eardrums in the process. Every instruction given by me was taken personally and inevitably not followed. I lost count of the number of times she claimed to have completed an activity in class, and on being told that she'd actually only done one-quarter of what she was asked, sneered at me with malicious intent. If looks could kill, I would truly be dead. She wasn't the only female student at Slothwick capable of spitting poison, but she was the best. On our trip to the Old Town, as we came upon the aforementioned coffin, Laurette asked: 'What will happen if I throw my pen at that coffin?' (like another mad bitch had done the previous day). My response was to ask her if she had life insurance.

Laurette: 'What does that mean?'

Me: 'It means I will kill you.'

Laurette: 'I'll kill you first.'

Me: 'Wanna bet?'

At this point in the stand-off, Vaughan rounded the corner to witness the splendid professionalism of his colonial import. And, with a few weeks left in the country at the time, guess who couldn't give a frog's fat arse?

Laurette wasn't the only one to cop it from both barrels in the last month of my stay. Another student who made my blood boil was a Year 8 called Richie Rhodes, or 'B cubed'[2] as I liked to call him. Richie was one of those filthy little snots who got his kicks out of spitting on stairs, railings and passing heads. He was very devious and rather unpopular for it, but managed to survive each day by cleverly surrounding himself with a gaggle of giggling cronies who were big enough to save him from having his head separated from his neck. Physical retribution was not an option for me, so I had to get him in other ways. As the months progressed, it wasn't uncommon for a conversation such as this to take place in my classroom:

'Richie Rhodes, stay in for detention!'

'Wha' for?'

'Because I don't like you.'

Richie was a pale, anaemic-looking, spindly-limbed, seemingly malnourished little urchin who had seen very little sun in his time on this planet. Imagine a young Mr Bean or, even better, Eddie Munster. Almost every morning, as my two colleagues and I drove up to the school, we would see him hanging around the bike shed and, unable to remember the Munsters' theme song, we settled for a couple of choruses of the next best thing—'The Addams Family' (Da da da da, tse tse…)

The bike shed itself made me laugh. Located next to the car park, this structure consisted of a brick wall, a corrugated iron roof and some barbed-wire fencing, clearly thrown together by the designer of Nazi death camps. I routinely referred to it as Auschwitz, and, after taking a photo of it, proceeded to insert the photo into my album and caption it 'Auschwitz'. Testament to its disturbing appearance is the number of people who have gazed on my photo and said: 'Wow! Did you go to Auschwitz?' Anyway, for reasons best known to him, Richie and one or two companions (who seemed to follow a roster), chose to hang out in the bike

---

[2] Beelzebub in a Boy's Body.

shed each morning before school, in direct contravention of school rules. Our game, as my contract neared completion, was to ask Richie to leave the area in the funniest way possible. 'Grow wheels or get out!' was my best effort and, desperate to outdo me, my colleague and friend Richard delivered on another occasion: 'If you're going to stay there Richie, at least bend over so we can park another bike.' 'Wha'?' was generally the best retort Munster could muster.

It was not difficult to identify the origin of the distinct lack of panache among Slothwick students. Their fathers had been known to roll up to Parent–Teacher Evenings on hot nights wearing nothing but a pair of jeans. When it was suggested to them that this might be a tad inappropriate, the response was generally the indignant 'Wha?!' (a term seemingly for all seasons). These were the sorts of blokes who would sit down at my interview table with a steely glare—one which suggested that I was about to cop a right royal grilling. So, I would spend the next three minutes giving a carefully worded but accurate account of their child's progress (or lack thereof), dotting all the i's and crossing all the t's (unlike their children) so as to head off any potential challenge. The response became predictable after a while: 'So, he's alright then?' 'Yes,' I would reply and that would wrap up the interview. Once I realised that this was all they wanted to hear, I could get through all the interviews in well under a minute, and then twiddle my thumbs for four. The attitude (among the parents at least) is simple—just like doctors, dentists and mechanics, teachers are professionals who know what they're doing.[3] Well not always.

[3] I must say, I was astounded and impressed by the proportion of parents who attended nights like this. In Australian public schools, ten per cent is a good result, and rarely are they the parents to which you really need to talk. At Slothwick, consistently more than eighty per cent of parents showed up, and I would be forced to turn many away! In hindsight, maybe they had nothing better to do. They did live in Stevenage after all.

Roland Graham was a Year 10 student who is, frankly, barely human. Although never personally having had a run-in with him, I knew all the stories. He was frequently suspended for periods of between one and fifteen days for all manner of offences—bullying, violence, abuse of staff, etc. His mother, Mandy, headed the cleaning team at the school. She was not a great deal older than her son and a heavily suspected, though never proven, thief. When the Head Teacher met with her one day to explain that Roland was to be permanently excluded from the school, her response was:

'You can't do this to us. I know my rights. I've seen this on *Brookside!*' (a popular soapie).

At one point, the school employed Alphonse, a guy from Guinea, to teach religious education. This man's gentle nature, along with his fairly poor English, set him up as a lamb ready for slaughter. Besides, anyone attempting to teach compulsory RE in an environment such as this deserves a Victoria Cross. Forcing sixteen year olds to learn about different religions in an increasingly secular society is, in my humble opinion, a recipe for disaster. Alphonse was battling with an even scarier culture shock than me and he was on the ropes. The school's leaders knew this but, desperate for staff as they were, they could do precious little about it.

As luck would have it, Alphonse's classroom was opposite mine. If those walls could talk, boy would they have a few stories. Routinely, I would be called upon to eject from my room Alphonse's students who were trying to escape others on a maniacal rampage, or who had come crashing through the door mid-rumble. It later emerged that Alphonse thought he needn't bother reporting the fact that four Year 9 boys had, on different occasions, clocked him one on the jaw. (You thought I had only metaphorically referred to him being 'on the ropes'.) This must have taken some courage on their part, for Alphonse was built like a brick shithouse! Apparently, our friendly cleaner

Mandy also fancied herself at a title shot and planted a right in his breadbasket. She was objecting, it seems, to being told that she should actually *clean* the classroom. Even the most fastidious of us (and I wish I had a dollar for every time I've been called 'anal') will occasionally miss a pen or bit of paper under a desk when tidying up. Apparently, Mandy had instructed all her 'girls' to teach us teachers a lesson by placing any rubbish they found on the teacher's desks. Who says teachers aren't respected? Could you imagine this happening to a company CEO, a legal partner or a politician?

The rule is simple: If you're after the basic respect of your fellow humans, don't become a teacher. One day I was called upon to eject from the school grounds three members of 'tha Hillview Massiv', Hillview being one of Stevenage's estates. These gents were clearly under the influence and roaming the school causing trouble. As I approached them from fifty metres they were sizing me up with lines like: 'Who's this fella?' I had no idea what I was going to do when I reached them, being fully aware of the power-lessness of teachers in this situation and the emptiness of the 'We'll get the police' threat, but I was so battle-hardened and stir crazy at this point that I didn't really care. Fortunately, my stride was assertive enough to convince them to move outside the school gate where they could prepare their insults for the Head Teacher and his deputies. Satisfied with the outcome, I turned and began to make my way back to the building. As soon as the distance between us was one hundred metres, the abuse started flying. In their situation, effectively beyond recrimination, I'm sure most of us could come up with a few pearlers. Not these chaps. The best they could come up with was 'Australian man'. It's strange, but coming from inmates of Stevenage, this didn't exactly cut me to the quick. But I didn't revel in it, unlike the Head of Technology, who had earlier felt the sting of 'Shut up, fat cock!' This was a description he accepted with considerable pride.

Cultural insensitivity is a theme that has underpinned much of this chapter. Try these ones out. Apparently in recent times, the school took a bunch of kids to an England versus West Indies cricket Test. When both teams were out on the field warming up, one lad turned to his teacher and asked: 'Which team is England?' Was this a comment on the success of the integration policies of the British Immigration Department? Or was it, as I suspect, another example of pure, unadulterated stupidity?

Barhey, a teacher at Slothwick, and as Indian as one could possibly look, was asked on one occasion if he was Welsh. Consequently, amongst his peers, he had no choice but to adopt the name 'Taffy'.

And then there's this little gem. Grace, my flatmate, and a teacher at the even more vile Buzzardsbeak School, was asked one day how long ago she had arrived in England from her native Canada. She replied that it had only been a week. 'Really?' said the student. 'How did you learn English so fast?'[4]

Against all odds, I returned to Australia after a year at Slothwick with my sanity relatively intact. I attribute this to three things.

The first is the camaraderie of my mates, the two Richards, with whom I travelled to and from work. In the car, every morning and every afternoon, we would revise targets and break up the weeks into smaller pieces in order to resuscitate our ailing morale. It's pretty sad to wish one's life away—it's usually a good sign that you

---

[4] I should mention here how gullible Grace herself could be every now and again. Once, when Kevin (my other flatmate) and I were about to head off to the gym, I asked him if he had his nappy. 'What?' inquired Grace, for whose benefit the question had been originally asked. I responded defensively: 'All serious weight-trainers use a nappy!' Keeping the ruse going, Kev and I explained to her the need for some protection for the times when one's bowels fail to cope with an especially challenging weight. She was thoroughly disgusted, and it took her weeks (no doubt punctuated by some restless nights) before she got to the bottom (pardon the pun) of this little white lie.

need a change. For me, I knew the change would come when I returned to Australia. There was no light at the end of their tunnels, and I don't know how they coped. This day-to-day lunacy had, I guess, become normal to them. I don't think they really knew that there are greener pastures. (Unlike other Australian teachers I met, I tried to refrain from rubbing their noses in the relative benefits of our situation.) Despite occasional lapses into the depths of depression, the three of us were quite successful in pep-talking our way through the week. We invented our own names for the days of the week. There was 'Miserable Monday'— we couldn't think of a way of dressing that up, except that we were closer to Friday than we had been the night before. Tuesday was 'Nothing'—it didn't deserve a name. Wednesday was 'The Hump'—it was all down hill once you got over it. Wednesday afternoon (after the bell went) had its own name. It was 'The Sniff'—the first sniff of the weekend. Thursday was 'Friday Eve', and Friday itself was, obviously, 'Fabulous Friday'.

The second thing to which I attribute my survival is alcohol. I challenge anybody to remain teetotal when working in a British comprehensive. Furthermore, pubs form the nucleus of British social life, and it is very difficult to stay out of them. Being in a pub and not drinking is like being in a restaurant and not eating. In the end, you just drink. I consumed alcohol in far greater quantities than I ever had before and, I'm certain, ever will again. After five days of sobriety, Fridays brought sweet release, and I was usually pissed before dinner. I knew that if I didn't make the most of my weekends, my life would cease to be worth living.

And the third thing that saved me…holidays.

Two
Ireland: My First Escape

Time restraints had seen this destination fall off the itinerary of my previous European adventure. Having spent a week there now, I've promised myself that I'll return.

Ireland is a unique place in all the ways that I had expected—the rolling green hills, the quaint rock walls, the cosy pubs, the chatty locals and their 'brogue-ish' way of speaking. There are some minor scenic wonders that are worth a look, such as the Cliffs of Moher and the Giants Causeway, but one doesn't go to Ireland for them. One goes (or at least I went) for the relaxed friendly lifestyle, for the stories, for the songs, and for the beer—for the 'vibe' of the place.

I was travelling with an Australian named Mark, a friend of a friend, and an acquaintance of mine because he had been my travel agent. A giant of a man and handy full forward in his day, Mark is happiest with a beer in one hand and a 'cancer stick' in the other, and he's pretty quick to spot 'bullshit'. His relaxed nature made him an amiable and accommodating travel partner.

After a late arrival one Sunday evening, the two of us headed out the next day to wander the streets of Dublin. Christ Church Cathedral and St Stephen's Green were pleasant but didn't exactly blow our minds. Dublin Castle is the most uncastle-like castle I've ever seen. If you're ever there, have a look, but only because you'll probably be walking straight past it. One bonus that day was paying a meagre four punts (Irish pounds) to get an eyeful of the amazing *Book of Kells* at Trinity College. Produced by the monks of Iona (an island off Scotland) in the ninth century and residing in Dublin since the seventeenth, it is ornate in the extreme and is one of those rare items that literally takes your breath away. One of the four volumes left Ireland for only the fourth time in 2000 and travelled to the National Gallery of Australia in my hometown of Canberra. On arriving at the gallery in that year and being told that I would need to line up for sixty to ninety minutes *after* paying, and that I would be able to look at it for less than a minute, I chucked a little tanty and left, believing I'd never see it. Here I was in Dublin and there was hardly anybody there. This was an unexpected highlight and there were more to come.

Our guidebook suggested we check out a pub called Kavanagh's, a.k.a. Gravediggers, next to Dublin's Glasnevin Cemetery. The cemetery itself is impressive, containing 1.2 million graves, including those of the Joyce family. But we went for a beer and it didn't take us long to find one. Besides, we had an excuse for starting to drink at midday. The second of my Canadian flatmates, Kevin, had been unable to get a seat on our flight and so had booked one for the following day. His flight was due to arrive any minute and Gravediggers was our appointed meeting place. We figured that a pub was a good place to meet because if the flight was delayed, we'd have something productive to do while we waited.

Have you ever met one of those complete wankers who, when drinking a pint of Guinness, will insist on interrupting your yawn to tell you that it tastes appreciably better in Ireland? Sadly, having tasted the Guinness at Gravediggers, I have become one of those wankers. You'll hear people say the stuff 'doesn't travel well'. That might be true—I wouldn't have a clue. But what I can tell you is that it is smoother and creamier than any Guinness I've tasted before or since. I had only started drinking Guinness a couple of months before I arrived in Ireland, and I certainly picked the right time to convert. The sad thing is that at my thirtieth birthday party in England, which happened to coincide with St Patrick's Day festivities at a local pub, I was lured centre-stage to skull a yard glass (equivalent to four and a half pints) of the famous beverage. I remember saluting the crowd on completion, I remember making it to the toilets (not to vomit, apparently some feat), and I remember making it on to a bench in Hitchin Town Square. What I don't recall is being supported by my noble friends for a thirty-minute 'walk' to my bed because no taxi would take me. Apparently, I was the epitome of dead weight. I haven't been able to touch a drop of 'The Black Death' since, but I'm determined to jump back on the horse one day, albeit in a far more mature fashion. When I was in southern China in 2000, I found myself involved in a rice wine drinking session with a regional schools director—the incomparable Mr Su. At one point, to my enduring pleasure, he leaned over to me and said: 'In China, if you drink a lot, you are a hero...' and, pointing to himself with real conviction, '... I am a hero'. I did not feel anything like a hero that night in Hitchin. In truth, I felt lucky to be alive. I suspect Mr Su was speaking as a man who had never attempted to neck a yard of Guinness.

Dublin's Gravediggers pub has barely changed since 1833, and you can still see the hole in the wall through which the bar staff once passed pints of Guinness to the thirsty graveyard shovellers. The décor is bland to say the least—a few wooden carrels which make it hard to know how many people are actually in there. There is no music and few pictures. Women are rarely sighted, and Mark and I were the youngest patrons by about fifteen years (though it is possible that some of the regulars were younger than they appeared, courtesy of a few too many drinking sessions). This is a real old-fashioned pub and if less is more, then this pub is a lot. Mark, not being a Guinness drinker, ordered a Harp lager (which is actually made by the Guinness company). After a quizzical look, the barman disappeared through a door into a kind of annex before emerging three minutes later with a pint of the stuff. Clearly, Mark's ilk is not common in this place. Most British and Irish pubs have a fairly comprehensive food menu and, as we were a little peckish, we thought we'd ask what was available.

'We have a cheese sandwich,' said the barkeep.

'Oh really. Anything else?' I asked.

'Let me see…we have a cheese and tomato sandwich.'

We got the picture. 'We'll take two of your Number 2 thanks.'

And you know what? Even these were bloody good.

It was a thoroughly enjoyable afternoon, made even more enjoyable by the fact that Kevin's flight was five hours late. (No offence to Kev intended.) By the time he arrived, we were pretty much as pissed as trough lollies and Kev had a lot of catching up to do. But he doesn't mind a challenge, so after downing a Guinness and putting up with twenty minutes of our dribble, he was persuaded to help us launch an assault on the infamous Temple Bar district of central Dublin. 'The Craic' is Irish for good times, and this was our first night on it.

From what I was able to gather, the Irish are quite different from the British. They seem somehow less inhibited, more playful and more spontaneous. For me, this is illustrated by the impromptu jam sessions that take place in pubs everywhere. Professional, semi-professional, amateur and hack musicians fuse regularly—by day or by night—to entertain anyone who is prepared to listen. What makes this practice different from karaoke, among other things, is that everyone seems to know what they're doing. Everyone in the pub can sing, shout, stamp and clap in time with the punchy toe-tapping tunes, and when the ballads are performed, the local butcher sings with the sort of heart that makes you want to slit your throat in sympathy. I'm always intrigued by the fact that some cultures seem to be more inherently musical than others. Take the Welsh. When they sing at the rugby, it actually sounds good. The whole bloody crowd can sing! This is a rare thing from my experience. I would say the Irish and the Welsh seem more musical than the English, yet England spawned the Beatles. The British—and of course the Americans—seem to strike a more universal chord with the music they produce, and Irish music, along with Welsh choir singing, remains something of an alternative or niche market. Perhaps power, money and marketing have a lot to do with it. If Ireland had achieved political, economic and military dominance the world over, as Britain and then the US did, would our best-loved pop stars be Irish? Popular culture is incredibly transportable and influential, and Australians, presently under the American spell, should recognise this fact all too well.

I can say this about the Irish: they are a friendly lot. Generally, they delight in conversation and it's as if their accent was made for a good chat. Ireland is still a place where you can talk to people—barmen, petrol station attendants, shopkeepers—and not feel as though you are taking up their precious time. This is part of its charm.

In the morning, after a big greasy breakfast, we left Dublin and took our hire car north in search of Newgrange. This is reputed to be one of the most impressive prehistoric sites in Europe and it didn't disappoint. Every winter solstice (22 December), for exactly seventeen minutes, the sun streams in through a tunnel to the heart of the structure. Like Stonehenge, Newgrange acts as an elaborate timepiece. The magnificently preserved five thousand year old burial tomb is a genuine marvel, as is the ancient stonework.

That afternoon we crossed Ireland from east to west before bunking down at lively Galway. We reached as far north as Sligo the next night before making Donegal the day after. All of these towns are quaint, look like they've been there since Adam was a boy and, we imagined, are typically and adorably Irish.

The guidebook we had featured numerous 'Top 10' lists—the Top 10 Irish Attractions, the Top 10 Museums, the Top 10 Castles, the Top 10 Pubs, the Top 10 Chicks (not really), and so on. By day four, all three of us had become completely obsessed with the idea of ticking off as many of the Top 10 as possible in *just about* every category. (Regrettably, we couldn't afford to sample the Top 10 restaurants.) We would leave the highway and drive for fifteen minutes just to get a look at castle #9, or we'd force food into our full bellies just so we could say we'd eaten at café #4. And Kev, usually from our backseat headquarters, would provide regular bulletins on our progress.

'We've had a drink at pubs 1, 2, 3, 5, 7 and 9, and we've been to attractions 1, 3, 4 and 6.' None of us saw how ridiculous this was at the time. I knew I was anal, I suspected Kev might be a fraction anal, but Mark was surprisingly, almost refreshingly, anal. It was funny anal. At least it provided a focus for our meanderings.

Donegal Castle was very cool and had the added advantage of being #6 (tick). The castle was owned by an Irish family until the early seventeenth century, when the English made it theirs. Once again, I was overwhelmed by the cruelty of which colonists have been, and still are, capable. The pattern throughout world history is unmistakable—just about every conquering imperial power has ruled with an excess of violence and malevolence. A genuine fear of reprisals explains some of this but self-interest and intolerance have surely played even greater parts. I was reminded of one of my favourite quotes, by Lord Acton: '[A]bsolute power corrupts absolutely'. I can't see many things destroying the amazingly resilient and resourceful human race, but greed (or maybe a bloody big meteorite) could do it.

I had cause for further historical and political musings as we crossed the virtually non-existent border (something which surprised me) into British-ruled Northern Ireland. I must admit that Northern Ireland had, for me, always seemed a place to avoid. In fact, prior to this trip, my mother in Australia had asked if I was going there and, to put her at ease, I had replied in the negative—a little white lie. (Sorry Mum.) Mark was dead keen to go, as he had heard that the black taxi tours of Belfast provided a real buzz. And as he worked in the travel industry, who was I to argue? Kev, who had once taken his white skin, blue eyes and flowing blonde locks for a jog in Soweto, would have agreed to pretty much anything.

Northern Ireland, as it turns out, is just like the rest of the island with the exception of certain areas like those in Derry (or Londonderry, depending on whom you'd like to offend) and the capital Belfast. No tourist has ever been killed in sectarian clashes and one's chances of being harmed by terrorism are statistically lower than they are in London. As an outsider, it is a precarious exercise to even begin to explain the situation in the troubled cities of the North. But after just a few days there, and some reading in the following weeks, I'm convinced of one thing. The majority of people in Northern Ireland want an end to the violence and are content to cohabit peacefully with those of either religion. The small, hard-core elements that are intent on prolonging hostilities are like this because they see 'The Troubles' as providing some purpose to their lives. These are people who feel the need to hate, and history is often distorted (or at least viewed selectively), to fuel this hate. Hopefully in years to come this minority will continue to shrink and cooler heads will prevail.

Walking the walls of Derry—a mile-long circuit around the elevated town centre—was an unforgettable experience. Peering over a wall to see a machine gun peering back at you reminds you of how serious things are in this volatile precinct. On one side is Bogside, the main nationalist (Catholic) area, with its distinctive green, white and orange street markings. On murals, defiant Catholics are depicted standing up to the force of British tanks, while on walls graffiti appears such as: 'The desire for freedom is a flame which can't be extinguished.' On the other side of the town centre is Waterside, the loyalist (Protestant) heartland. Its street markings are the familiar red, white and blue of Great Britain, and its murals and slogans are just as passionate. On one wall, we read: 'Londonderry West Bank Loyalists—still under siege, no surrender.' Although somewhat wary the whole time, we were relaxed enough to fully appreciate the unique nature of this place (and purchase some irresistibly cheap socks at the nearby markets).

Our plan in Belfast was to drive in, do a black taxi tour, drink a pint in the Crown Liquor Saloon (#5) and get the hell out. We were lucky enough to find a willing taxi driver fairly quickly. The guy, in his mid-twenties, seemed to be licking his lips at scoring the gig. At the time I thought it was because he was going to profit handsomely from driving three tourists round town for an hour and a half. It soon became clear, though, that he was thrilled to have the chance to scare the shit out of a few dopey blow-ins. He took us to all the hotspots, such as Protestant Shankill Road, with its aggressive murals and seemingly deserted estates. There were no kneecap shootings on this particular afternoon, but they do happen. As I've read since, it is not uncommon for members of one side to request the attendance of one of their supposed allies at an appointed time and place (often on Shankill Road). The victim, whose offence is usually that he has become a bit too big for his boots, is shot in the calves if lucky, or the kneecaps if unlucky. He can kiss goodbye to walking if the latter fate befalls him.

Catholic Falls Road was next, with its tense atmosphere and history of execution-style killings. Then came the 'Peace Line', a wall that divides the two areas. At each place, our taxi driver would invite us to leave the taxi, take photos and even wander down the street and meet him at the other end. He informed us, with a straight face, that if we heard gunfire we should stay low and dive back into the taxi. He was loving it! He was, to be sure, very knowledgeable and satisfyingly objective—unlike, I understand, some of his competitors. Some taxi companies are owned and run by those of one religion alone. You can imagine the slant they'd put on things. Our driver told us upfront that he was Protestant, but that he had Catholic friends. The experience of being in (and out of) his taxi was undoubtedly one of my most memorable of the trip. I'm grateful to Mark for suggesting it.

Arriving back in Dublin, we remembered that we wouldn't be able to face our mates unless we'd made the pilgrimage to the Guinness Brewery. Apparently, the tour once led you through the large wooden vats and associated machinery, giving you a real taste for the day-to-day operations of arguably the world's most identifiable brewery. Several millions of dollars later, the place has become a series of modern, sterile exhibits only marginally eclipsing drying paint in the interest stakes. Yes, you do receive a pint once you reach the top floor but, after paying the exorbitant entrance fee and making your way up all the floors, you'd bloody well want to. In fairness, the top floor bar does provide a fantastic view over Dublin. A tip: just go to the merchandise section on the bottom floor. The shop is free to enter, and its range and affordability make it probably the best souvenir shop I've ever seen (my #1). Hopefully you can talk your way out of joining the frustratingly long queue.

That brought us to our final afternoon in Ireland. What to do...what to do...the decision was unanimous. Back to Gravediggers. Well we had to go! A mate of Mark's, Ben (with whom we were crashing the night), had never been there, and, as semi-regulars, we felt that it was our duty to take him.

This time I got talking to the barman; as lovable an Irishman as you'd meet. He started telling me about his distance running and, as someone who likes a bit of a trot myself, I showed a genuine interest. This bloke ran his first marathon at the age of forty-two and in the following twenty years has managed to find time to run another one hundred and sixty. He has run all over the world and has even completed the ninety-kilometre Comrades Marathon in South Africa. I recalled this race because it gave rise to one of the greatest cheating displays of all time. In 1999, the winner (one of the Motsoeneng brothers) was found to have run only part of the race. The remainder was run by his identical twin. They almost got away with it, but were found out because, as photographs revealed, they'd worn their wristwatches on different arms. Anyway, this guy behind the bar, by his tenacity and longevity, seemed to give us all hope—even mugs like me. The secret, he said, was a pint of Guinness before every race. (I made up that bit.)

My newfound friend was impressed enough with my take on life to invite me to sign the Gravediggers visitors book. It was a Saturday, and I noticed that this ancient relic (the book, not the barman) hadn't been dragged out since the Wednesday. On that particular occasion, he'd asked Pierce Brosnan to sign it. Pierce had apparently been working on a film in the adjacent cemetery and had popped in for a beer. And as he'd signed off with the trademark '007', I felt obliged to add '008' to my name. At least that put us both in the Top 10—we wouldn't have known what to do without our rankings! One individual that didn't merit a ranking was Brosnan's co-star Glenn Close. She'd been in on the Thursday, but had not been asked to sign the book on account of the fact that she was allegedly a 'boring deadshit'.

The next day, after having visited twenty of the thirty-two counties and leaving most of the south for another time, we boarded our flight back to England. It was time to give the liver a break.

Three
Spain and Portugal:
Exploring the Contiki Myth

I was a little worried about my thirteen-day Contiki tour to the Iberian Peninsula.

These tours, designed and heavily patronised by antipodeans, and marketed for eighteen to thirty-fives, had never interested me before. In 1997, I'd explored Europe with my long-time girl-friend, Marina. The freedoms of independent travel appealed to us then, and they still appeal to me now. To be able to set your own targets and change them as you go is a fantastic thing. If you like a Tuscan village, you can stay an extra couple of nights. If the weather is poor, leave early. Find a good café in Paris and catch a later train. You know what I mean. I met a guy who'd done ten Contikis and he told the story of a woman who had done twenty! (Apparently, the company had thrown in her twenty-first for free.) I could never do that. To me, it's like never taking the train-ing wheels off your bike. To have to find your own way around is character building, and it is extremely rewarding to stray from the beaten track. After doing this Contiki, however, I realised that there is a place for these tours.

As I see it, there are five reasons why you would consider doing a Contiki tour or the like:

1. To give you a taste of a large area if time is short.
2. To mitigate the considerable dangers and annoyances of inde-pendent travel in certain parts of the world (especially if you are a woman).
3. To see an expensive region (Scandinavia, for example) at a reasonable price. (The tours are generally pretty good value.)
4. You are simply too lazy to do anything and would like to be

ferried from hotel to hotel, or from camping ground to camping ground, without lifting a finger.

5. To surround yourself with a group of like-minded young people whose countries you can learn about. (Some might be persuaded to join you in a beverage or two, and others to become acquainted with your loins.)

This final reason is really the only one I'm prepared to accept for doing a Contiki tour of Western or Central Europe. This part of the world is so traveller-friendly that you can do it on your ear.

This same reason inspired me to sign up for Spain and Portugal. It was the Christmas holidays, my English mates were with their families (and the idea of being a tag-along didn't turn me on) and, after another soul-destroying seven-week stint at Slothwick, I needed to let my hair down.

But I'd heard the stories. 'Shagtiki', where you were forced to fornicate several times a day with anything that wasn't nailed down, or 'Grogtiki', where you had to drink yourself into oblivion and wake up in a pile of your own vomit. At twenty-nine, I was worried about being left behind by the youngsters. But, as you know, I had been getting some training—drinking more than fornicating—and, come the eve of the tour, I felt that I might be able to match it. Up my sleeve also was the experience gained over several years of end-of-season trips with the infamous Kingston Wolves (an Australian Rules football club no longer in existence). Here I witnessed acts too unspeakable for the pages of this book. On second thoughts, there's very little that I regard as unspeakable...

The Almanac of Kingston Wolves' Antics, a book which is crying out *not* to be written, would undoubtedly be subtitled *The Life and Times of Feds*. The archetypal larrikan, 'Feds' has consistently raised the bar of misbehaviour at events involving the service of alcohol. From his persistent interjections of 'Too drunk to fuck!' at a formal presentation dinner, to his daring urination facing a busy highway, Feds has astounded all and sundry in footy circles and earned for himself something of a cult hero status. One year, our new coach was attending his first post-season trip and, on the bus journey, attempted to impress us with stories of his drinking prowess and juvenile hijinks. Delivered within earshot of the dormant Feds, this was a schoolboy error. Within hours of arriving at the hotel and, to his eventual and eternal torment, being roomed with the incomparable Feds, coach Thommo was in for his first crisis. Making a trip to the bathroom, he discovered that his toothbrush had been smeared with poo-poo. There were no prizes for guessing the culprit. I'll never forget Thommo's reaction to this (for him) near apocalyptic event. Curled up on the couch in a position approaching foetal, he debriefed, bubbling the following:

'The man...does not comprehend...the basic principles...of human behaviour...'

Feds, it seems, had taken another scalp and, in the process, changed me forever. As long as I live, it will take a fair bit to shock me.

To my surprise, early form was pretty ordinary amongst the Contiki group, and I thought I might have my work cut out to get more than a few to go out on the town. Sure, there looked to be a handful of potential party-goers, but I was looking like benchmark material. I was chuffed—the pressure was off.

A core group emerged, along with several splinter groups, and there was always someone to go out with of an evening. A familiar pattern emerged as we wound our way south from Madrid. Dine, drink and dance till 4.00 a.m., rise and shine at 6, on the road by 7, walk around sites like a zombie till 5, powernap for an hour, apply the aftershave and do it all again. Despite my state of semi-consciousness, I was as entranced by Spain as anyone. And the place needed to redeem itself for me. In 1997, I couldn't get out fast enough.

Barcelona, my only previous Spanish destination, seems to have a peculiar effect on travellers. Nobody I've talked to remembers

Barcelona as being 'okay' or 'quite nice'—they either adore it or abhor it. There's no doubt that Antonio Gaudi's architecture and the street performers on La Rambla (the main pedestrian strip) have worked their charm on many a satisfied visitor, but I've found the horror stories to be just as prevalent. Take the case of a Sydney couple I know.

Jacquie and James picked up their hire car in Avignon, France and, after two days of fairly harrowing driving (James was a first-timer in a left-hand drive and had, unthinkingly, asked for a manual gearbox), started to make their way into the metropolis of Barcelona. Fooled by the city's grid system and stopped at traffic lights wondering where they were, they suddenly noticed a young man at the front of the car, pointing excitedly at the headlights. Simultaneously, another man crept up from behind the car, opened the driver's door and hauled James out. (At this point in the story, I would like you to imagine a soundtrack of Jacquie screaming at the top of her lungs.) Flipping the boot, the punks, whose number had now swelled to six, began helping themselves to the luggage. For some reason, they coupled this with bouncing on the car. Finding two of the three bags too heavy to run with, and probably becoming slightly flustered by Jacquie's spine-chilling screams, the criminals left with the smallest of the three bags. Jacquie gave chase, before realising (with some help from James), the madness of her actions. A stocktake revealed that passports and other valuables, which had been in the stolen bag for the previous ten days, were actually in the glove box on account of the fact that they had just been through border checks. More good news— most of what they had lost was cycle-wear, and, after ten days of hugging James as he cycled through France, these garments stank to high heaven. For the six shitheads, this was hardly 'the mother lode'. Taking heart in this fact, Jacquie and James believed that their four-day visit could go ahead as planned. Finally spotting their hotel, they pulled up at another set of traffic lights nearby…when who should they see running frantically down the footpath in their direction? THE BOYS! And, after getting a whiff of James' unwashed bike togs, this time it was personal! The lights turned green and James darted down an alley. As he passed the crims, he noticed that they were laughing. He soon found out why. He had entered a dead-end alley. Doing a U-turn, he was soon moving back up the street. Within seconds, all six of them had jumped on to the car. By now, James had had enough. He put the foot down, hooning up the street, clipping a parked car and dislodging the six articles of human baggage. In a flash, he was safely through a red light and, minus a hotel deposit, out of the city.

Thinking that they should report this to the police—for insurance purposes if nothing else—our heroes stopped at a little Spanish town. Unable to locate a police station, they soon found themselves in an outpost of the Spanish National Guard. Here, in an interrogation chamber, they attempted to explain what had been stolen to the supposed English expert, who could barely manage 'Hello'. A marathon game of charades ensued, in which the terms 'swimming goggles' and 'mobile phone charger' proved the most challenging. Perhaps understandably, Jacquie and James have since blacklisted Spain.

My Barcelona experience in 1997 wasn't much better. After a day being hassled by beggars (at a time when I wasn't accustomed to it), I walked with Marina to the Columbus Monument, near the port. On arrival, we heard a loud skidding noise followed by an almighty bang. Looking in the direction of the commotion, we saw that a bus had hit a young woman. She was one hundred metres away, and, as the area was full of people (including a bus full of passengers), I never dreamed that I would be the first one to her aid. As I arrived, bending down to remove a piece of chewing gum that was obstructing her breathing, I was shoved out of the way by some clown who appeared to be a traffic cop. As a crowd formed, he began to perform his own special brand of first aid on the injured woman, holding on to her ankles and flapping her legs up and down in slapstick fashion. The bus driver, seeing that his job was on the line, thought he'd better help out by doing the same with her arms. Until an ambulance arrived, she was like a puppet on a string. The situation was a farce the likes of which Monty Python would have been proud, but at the time, it was extremely distressing. We left, hoping that she survived, and thanking our lucky stars that we weren't in America, where we would probably be having our arses sued for being a party to this debacle.

Next stop was a local beach, at which I promptly became locked in a toilet cubicle, screaming at the café staff for my release. Eventually I risked further embarrassment by crawling out through the small gap under the door. Thankfully, nobody saw me. Could this day get any worse? Answer: Yes.

Hoping to put things behind us, we planned a relaxing after-noon ride on the funicular (sky-car) at Montjuich. Here I walked through the wrong gate (an easy thing to do if you don't read Spanish), a move that apparently invalidated my ticket. Given that nobody was around, I hoped the attendant would give me a break, open the gate for me to come back out, and allow me to go in the correct gate. Flexibility and compassion not forthcoming, I was forced to fly into a rage and hurl my thick guidebook at a nearby wall. By this time an English-speaking couple had arrived, wit-nessed the unfairness with which I'd been treated and given me a spare ticket which, also confused, they had unwittingly bought. I thanked them politely before telling the bloke behind the counter that he could shove his funicular 'right up his fat one'. We adjourned to the hotel to pack.

I generally leave places with many more amusing stories than miserable ones. I have only one Barcelona story that gets me giggling. In a taxi on the way to the train station, our driver, to his credit, tried to make conversation with us in English.

Taxi driver: 'Where you go now?'

Me: 'To Nice.'

Taxi driver: 'Yes, but where you go to now?'

Me: 'Nice.'

Taxi driver: 'You catch train now?'

Me: 'Yes.'

Taxi driver: 'Where you catch train to?'

Me: 'Nice.'

Taxi driver: 'Where to?'

Me: 'Nice, in France.'

Taxi driver: 'Where in France?'

Me: 'Nice.'

Taxi driver (using his hands to draw a map): 'From here...Barthelona...to here...??'

Me: 'Nice.'

Taxi driver (light bulb appearing): 'Ahh, Neetha. Nice place.'

If you do go to Barcelona, practise your Spanish 'c'. You'll need to, because beer is *cerveza*—'thervetha'.

It was early days, but this time round I was thoroughly enjoying my Spanish experience. This didn't surprise me, aware as I was that the Catalans of Barcelona are notably different to other Spaniards and see themselves in that light. The old Spanish capital, Toledo, is a photographer's dream atop a hill in the turn of a river. It offers cobbled streets, beautiful crafts, a colossal cathedral and the art of El Greco, who earned my admiration for inserting a likeness of his illegitimate child into a painting of the funeral for a bloke he couldn't stand. Importantly, Toledo provided me with my first taste of Moorish architecture. From 711 to 1492, the Moors—Muslim Berbers and Arabs from North Africa— occupied various parts of the peninsula. Their influence can still be seen at our next stop, Cordoba. The Mosque of the Caliphs, with its brilliant red and cream internal arches, is only rendered imperfect by the sight of a bloody great Christian church that has been stuck in the middle of it. No such vandalism has taken place at Granada's Alhambra, the former residence of the Moorish kings and scene of their eventual defeat by the 'reconquering' Catholics in 1492. Here the mosaics are amazing, watched over for centuries by squatters who lived there after the Moors' expulsion. It was interesting to discover that the statues of animals at the palace had been sculpted by Jews. Muslims, I learned, are not permitted to recreate life—only Allah can do that.

Another humbling site in Granada is the church in which Isabelle and Ferdinand, Spain's unifying monarchs and sponsors of its Golden Age of exploration, are buried. Atop their tomb is a stone edifice depicting the couple at rest. The sculptors believed Isabelle to be the real brains of the partnership, and showed this by having her head sitting deeper in the pillow. Nearby are the resting places of the previous Catholic rulers. Phillip the Handsome was apparently so handsome that, after his death, his wife slept with his corpse for three years. Her name was Joanna the Mad.

Our guide in Granada, Paolo, was thrilled to have us lining up to get a photo with him at the end of the tour. He'd been adequate, but not good enough to warrant a picture. We wanted the photo because he was an absolute dead ringer for American comic and actor Rodney Dangerfield (or Rod *Dongerfield* as we preferred).[5] Needless to say, the afternoon was spent inserting Rodney's lines from *Back to School* and *Caddyshack* into every possible opening. And like the latter film ended, so did our tour: 'Hey everybody! We're all gonna get laid!' Forever optimistic.

One head that all of this humour went over belonged to an interesting character called Ash. Hailing from outback Queensland, Ash was thirty-four and looked a hell of a lot older.

---

[5] I know I've already mentioned Rodney once in this book, but it is not an obsession, I promise. There's only one American actor with whom I have something of an obsession, and you'll have to read Chapter Nine to find out more.

He'd either had a hard life, a very good one, or both. Bearing a striking resemblance to Australian rock legend Ian Moss, it seemed only fair to refer to him as 'Mossy' for the majority of the trip. Mossy had never been anywhere. He had come into some money and decided to go to Ireland to see the homeland of his ancestors. At short notice, he couldn't get a plane ticket. Remembering that he had some Spanish blood in him from somewhere, he thought he'd give Spain a go, and was able to grab the last spot on the tour. We were privileged to be there at so many of his firsts. His first bus ride and first train ride followed his first plane ride. Foods that he'd never tasted, words that he'd never heard—he was like a kid in a candy store. On the bus one day, people were providing their 'porn names' (you know, the name of your first pet followed by the name of the first street you lived in). He couldn't do it because he'd never lived on a street. 'Where were you born?' someone asked. 'Out bush' was the reply. Another day he commented that there was 'a lot of buildin' goin' on around 'ere (central Spain)'. He seemed to think that this was somehow linked to the fact that 'there's not much goin' on up north (Queensland)'. He was the most lovably naive and humble guy I've ever met. I'd like to have him in my email address book, but I don't think he'd ever heard of email.

Mossy, like most of us, was keen for a big one on New Year's Eve at the Costa del Sol. This area I can imagine would be pretty tasteless in peak season, and it was downright dismal when we were there in winter. Still, I looked for the positives—I could wear shorts for the first time since March. The party was fun, though tempered slightly by the fact that beers were A$10 each. Our tour manager, Greg, assured us that it was the cheapest place around. In reality, it was undoubtedly the only place where he'd drink for free and receive a nice little kickback. Can't blame him for that—he's got to make a living. Plus, he made amends by getting a few too many free beers into his neck, getting his kit off and, in a disturbing move which he later claimed was his trade-mark, began licking his fingers and rubbing his nipples (á la Austin Powers). The look on his face of 'Ouch, that hurts!' was what amused me. It's captured on film.

Greg had a real passion for Spain and this came across in the knowledge he'd been able to retain. A bonus was the fact that he was hilarious without even trying. Each time he'd pick up the microphone in the bus to tell us something, he'd begin with a smoker's cough, followed by an 'excuse me'. It got to the point where, as soon we heard him pick up the mike, we'd beat him to it, coughing and saying 'excuse me'. We did this from the back of the bus, so he had no idea why everybody was laughing at him. Despite basing himself in London, Greg was as Aussie as they come. At Cordoba, he told the group that at 3.00 p.m. we were going to meet at the bus and then 'shoot through' (leave). Not surprisingly, two Japanese girls, struggling with even the Queen's English, misconstrued this piece of information and failed to make the meeting point. Contiki's policy is clear in matters such as this, so at 3.10 we were off. Miwa and Yoko, armed with their 'Get Lost Sheet', were able to catch a train and meet us at our hotel in Granada. Greg was not deterred by this incident and continued to use a myriad of Australianisms. For the quarter of the group that was Australian, this didn't present a problem. We were happy to translate for the rest. Thus, they knew what to do when he told them to 'leg it' (move quickly), that we had to get going at 'spar-row's fart' (very early) or that we should have a back-up plan for when 'things go pear-shaped' (plans fall through). I noticed a lot of confused facial expressions when he informed us that the Lisbon subway was 'a piece of piss' (uncomplicated). Greg was good mates with our Spanish bus driver, Milo, whose driving indicated that he was getting in some practice for the next 500cc motorcycle grand prix. (Somebody should have told him that buses have more than two gears.) Milo was also top value, happy to pose for us in front of the aptly-named 'Eurorutas' bus wearing my 'mullet' wig[6] and forming his fingers into the risqué 'barracuda'.

Gibraltar is a classic example of a place you go to so that you can say you've been there. I've been to Gibraltar now. I've seen the Rock. Next.

Seville is a brilliant place, quintessentially Spanish. Tapas bars are everywhere and the delicacies are mouth-watering, though I was somewhat disappointed with my 'seasonal fruits' at one eatery. I had expected a little more than two unpeeled mandarins and a knife and fork. Still, it seemed a safer option than the 'Sausage from Hell'. To me, that was one step away from 'The Turd of Satan' and I wasn't interested.

Seville, a former host city for the 1929 Americas Exposition (where Spain's ex-colonies exhibited) and the 1992 World Expo, boasts the third largest cathedral in Europe (the Giralda) and in it are said to be Columbus's remains (though this, apparently, is a dubious claim). It also has an enormous bullring, but I declined to enter—moral reasons of course. Besides, I'd already bought tickets to the bear baiting.

In all seriousness, I'm surprised that I was the only one out of a group of forty-eight people to make a stand (albeit a passive one) at the bullring. Previously, many had been disgusted by what they saw when they spent the daylight hours of New Year's Eve attending a bullfight at the little town of Mijas, just up from our hotel on the Costa del Sol. Here, in Spain's smallest bullring, they squirmed as rank amateurs took up to twenty attempts to complete

[6] I had procured this wig from a lady at a 'Heroes and Villains' party in London (which is discussed in Chapter Ten). She had arrived as cricketer Ian Botham, and kindly presented me with the wig when she saw how much I loved wearing it. She had shortened the sides of a standard wig, but left it long at the back, to create a very special 'mullet' effect. Mossy actually had a mullet, but didn't seem to be offended by my wearing of the wig. To be honest, I don't think he understood the joke.

the kill. (The best matadors can usually stick the bull in the correct spot—adjacent to the shoulder blades—first time.) If the Spanish are not prepared to ban this barbaric 'sport', they should at least make it a fair fight. Let's see the matador take on a bull that has not been bled previously to render it weak and drowsy.

I have since revisited my decision not to enter the bullring, wondering if perhaps, for the sake of educating myself, I should have had a look. After all, it was in the name of education that I chose to enter more despicable places, such as Dachau concentration camp, near Munich in Germany. I guess the difference, though, is that the evils of Dachau—and all of the dungeons and castles that I've seen—are in the past. Bullfighting is an evil that is still occurring, and I don't want to be seen as supporting it in any way. Following this thinking through, I now regret my refusal to see Hitler's 'Eagle's Nest' when I was in Austria, and one day I intend to rectify this.

At night in Seville, we attended a flamenco show. It was all pretty monotonous and ho-hum until a dancer I christened 'The Dark Side' entered the fray. You should have seen how intense this guy was, and he became more so when we took it upon ourselves to wind him up to the max. 'You the man!' we cried, as if he needed to be told that. Boy could he stamp that floor. Later on, a few of us stumbled upon a side door in town that took us into another flamenco show. This, though, was not put on for the tourists—it was the real McCoy. Feverish guitar picking, haunting vocals and some energetic footwork had us spellbound. The crowd, from what we could make out, comprised mainly local students. The exception was an American tourist who, of course, made a beeline for us. He was the sort of guy who gives Americans a bad name. He'd done everything that was worth doing and he was more than happy to tell us all about it.[7]

---

[7] People who want to tell you all about their travels—don't they make you sick!

He showed no interest in us whatsoever—we were merely an audience. I tuned out after a few minutes and left him with Mossy. I thought it was nice juxtaposition—a man who had done everything talking to a man who had done nothing. I hoped Mossy would start telling him about 'the buildin' up north'.

The next day we stopped to photograph the sixteenth century aqueduct at Elvas, before making our way to the Portuguese capital. Flattened by an earthquake in 1755, Lisbon has been almost totally rebuilt and is visually appealing. It has some good clubs too, but when it comes to times, these Latinos are crackers. Not only do the Portuguese and Spanish sleep in the middle of the day; if you turn up to dinner before 9.30 p.m. then you've suddenly got two heads. Clubs don't get going until after 11. It was an interesting experience to see the New Year in while being totally sober. Coming from Britain, where they kick you out at 11, a bit of adjusting was required.

In Lisbon, I had the second funniest drug dealer proposition of my life. A group of us were walking across the attractive city square at dusk, when I heard a sharp whistle behind me. It was the sort of whistle one would use on a dog. In fact, I assumed it was for a dog and, without turning around, kept walking. A couple of seconds later I heard it again, only this time it was closer. Curious by now, I turned and saw a guy in his twenties walking towards me, like he was in a real hurry. He looked piercingly into my eyes and, without stopping, asked aggressively: 'Hasheeesh?' He was rubbing his thumb against his index finger as if to indicate that he intended to charge me for it. I shook my head and he disappeared from my life as quickly as he had entered it. I was amused by his apparent assumption that I had an urgent need and that he was the man to satisfy that need, and that he could do it RIGHT NOW—but I had to be quick. It was very cloak and dagger.

Now that the previous story's preamble has presented the

opportunity for me to tell my funniest ever drug dealer proposition, I will happily do so. In 1997, Marina and I were strolling around the Red Light District of Amsterdam, gazing in wonderment at the (remarkably attractive) prostitutes in the windows and ignoring the advances of sex show touts. As we approached a bridge, I could see a guy pretending to mind his own business (when really he intended to mind ours), and I knew what was afoot. 'Here we go,' I said to Marina, and, sure enough, he delivered in a superbly laidback drawl:

'Some ecstasy…for the lovers…for the sex?'

There are numerous funny things about this offer. Firstly, there's the fact that he managed to pack four gross assumptions into an eight-word sentence. He assumed we took drugs (incorrectly), he assumed we were lovers (correctly), he assumed that we were sexually active (well…I just lied there actually, but correctly), and he assumed that our sex needed enhancing (you'll have to check with Marina, but I would say incorrectly). Then, (and I'm hoping you don't think I'm analysing this too deeply) there's his overuse of the word 'the'. We should have been flattered I guess. Apparently we weren't just lovers; we were 'the lovers'. And we were about to engage in 'the sex'. I laughed out loud when he said it, and then I watched my back.

Our last stop in Portugal was at Fatima. Here, in 1917, two children saw a holy vision of the Virgin Mary above a tree, and the site is now one of the most visited Catholic shrines in the world. People (mainly women from my observation), shuffle on their knees down a long slope to the scene of the famous vision, where they pause to pray. My only thought was that if they were really serious about this they'd shuffle *up* the slope. That I'd stay to watch.

Spain's Salamanca, home to one of the world's oldest universities (1227), is a wonderfully historical place. We were lucky enough to be there when a street carnival was in full swing; its sounds, colours and costumes were captivating. I wish we'd stayed longer, but regal Madrid beckoned.

After eleven of the thirteen days, I was forced to leave the group at the capital and head back to work. I never imagined that after such a short time, I would be emotional, but I was. The group clicked and friends for life were made. I still catch up with two of the Australian guys, Matt and John, each of whom have a sense of humour as twisted as mine. John, who insisted on being called 'Juan' whilst he was in Spain, managed to combine a stated desire to have sex with a woman from every country that he visited with an obsessive refusal to touch door handles for fear of contracting some sort of disease. I'm not sure he saw the irony in this.

There was a guy on the trip called Sean, who, Matt informed us after a moment of inspiration, looked like Jim Carrey's muppetesque character 'The Grinch'. Considering how unattractive The Grinch is, Sean (by no means hideous) was a good sport about his new tag. (His self-esteem was more than healthy, as demonstrated by his uncontrollable urge to take centre stage and strip off every time he heard 'Rock DJ' by Robbie Williams.) One day, we all hopped off the Eurorutas bus at a seaside town, and the bus moved away. What nobody knew was that The Grinch was actually in the bus' toilet at the time. Realising something wasn't right, he released the chocolate hostage, then released himself from the latrine and hollered at Milo to stop the bus. Running up the hill to join us, he probably thought that our collective fit of laughter would be the end of the matter. And it was…unless you count the fact that the term 'Grinch' was thereafter used to describe the bus toilet, any other toilet, the act of going to the toilet and even the excrement itself.

I really do recommend Contiki to young folk, particularly if they ever find themselves in circumstances such as mine. From talking to Greg, it seems that the stories I'd heard over the years were probably true, but that times have changed. The company apparently now takes a much harder line on antisocial or over-the-top behaviour. Furthermore, the groups seem to be getting older, according to Greg. Indeed, the average age on our trip was in the late twenties—not that we acted anywhere near that old.

Four
Egypt: 'Souvenirs, Novelties, Party Tricks...!'

I'd looked forward for a very long time to taking my first step on the African continent. Africa has long captured the imagination of novelists and filmmakers alike, and they in turn have captured the imaginations of so many of us. *King Solomon's Mines*, the *Biggles* stories and, more recently, *Indiana Jones* and Michael Crichton's *Congo* are just a few of the books and movies that have brought this continent alive for me. There's only one reason I hadn't gone prior to this visit—fear.

I wouldn't say I'm a complete nancy boy when it comes to hairy destinations. Like all serious travellers, I appreciate the value of a good culture shock here and there, and I have certainly felt mildly out of my depth in the past. I am also aware of the fact that I could be killed crossing the street outside my house. But I really don't think I'm going to enjoy myself in a place where there is anything more than a tiny chance of me actually kicking the bucket. It is a holiday after all.

In 1998, my flatmate Jacquie signalled her intention of doing a three-week safari through eastern and central Africa, culminating in a meeting with mountain gorillas in Uganda. This, along with a crossing of Ngorangora Crater (which, due to the nature of its creation, is a microcosm of the African landscape and positively teems with wildlife), was enough to see me seriously considering tagging along. A couple of months after first discussing the idea, we sat down one night to watch the news. Nineteen tourists, some of whom were Australian, had been murdered and mutilated by Hutu rebels. It turns out that one of Jacquie's best friends (who had provided the initial inspiration for the safari) had been in another group of travellers who had dined with the doomed group the night before the massacre. That was enough for us—Africa could wait.

South Africa is another place that bothers me. The idea of running red lights in Johannesburg (reputed to be the world's most dangerous city) in order to avoid being car-jacked turns me on about as much as taking a handgun on a family picnic (like my friend's family do near Durban). I'm always wary of places where a significant proportion of the population have very little to lose and are prepared to kill and die for their cause or for money. Another curveball was thrown by the events of 11 September 2001 and its aftermath. Many of my fancied African destinations are Islamic nations, and I felt that this needed to be taken into account.

Morocco was my main interest. A short flight from the UK and relatively stable in political and economic terms, this country offers the vibrant market towns of Fez and Marrakech, the legendary port of Casablanca and treks to Berber camps in the Atlas Mountains. The problem was that I only had one week (it was the February half-term break) and the dates of any tour needed to coincide. In the end, I was unlucky—it is clear that tour operators rarely consider teachers when they set their dates. This strikes me as silly, given the large number of young teachers I met travelling independently and on tours.

I started looking for alternatives. Top Deck tours, I discovered, offered a week-long 'Nile Discovery' tour and its dates matched mine. Egypt has had more than its share of tourist-related tragedies in recent times (on which I will elaborate later in the chapter), but my decision to sign up for this tour was a quick one. My thinking on the matter went a little bit like this: 'Stuff it!' Sometimes you've just gotta do things.

The fact that this was a brand new tour (and, I guess, word of mouth had not had time to spread) led to quite a strange situation. The group comprised myself and only five others. These five were close friends and Spanish speakers—three were from Spain and two from Colombia. Some lived and worked in London and all had a command of English to some degree. All of them were lovely people, and I got on particularly well with the two guys Rafa and Hendry (probably because I roomed with them), but I couldn't help feeling as though I was on the fringe. Our Egyptian guide, Hamada, had spent a lot of his time in Belgium due to a love interest. He was worldly, funny and bawdy, and these traits, along with the fact that he couldn't communicate in Spanish, meant that the two of us hit it off famously. His local knowledge served us well and, considering that I'd had to give him a spare copy of the itinerary on the second day so that we could progress, he did a sterling job as a guide. Hamada was actually part of the company's clerical staff. He'd been called in after the first day to replace a seemingly drugged-out, lazy dullard about whom complaints had been made. (At the Egyptian Museum, this guy, whose name escapes me, sat around a lot, answering most questions with a less than comforting 'I don't know'.)

As a heathen, most of my pilgrimages tend to be historical ones. And for history, there are few places that can compete with Egypt. First stop: the Pyramids of Giza, built in the twenty-seventh century BC. Of one hundred and nine pyramids that once adorned the Egyptian landscape, only seven are still standing, and all are in the Cairo area. Many tourists are stunned on arrival at the Pyramids to find that they are not in the middle of the desert (as one might imagine) but actually a stone's throw from Cairo's outer suburbs. I had been pre-warned and was therefore prepared for this.

Arriving at the largest of the three—the Great Pyramid of Khufu (or Cheops as the Greeks called him)—we were casually informed that we needed to be back on the bus in ten minutes. Ten bloody minutes!! We'd sat in the frickin' restaurant twiddling our thumbs for fifteen minutes while our account was haggled over, and now the aforementioned lazy dullard expected us to spend ten measly minutes at one of the most prominent landmarks on the planet! This is one of the downsides of tours I guess. I tried not to let it get me down. I thought that I could still escape the crowds and do a lap of the thing, gazing up and dreaming of times past. It was going to be a task—the stone blocks are absolutely enormous—but I was determined not to be distracted from my goal. It was then that I was confronted by some bloke riding a camel.

'Camel ride, sir?'

'No thanks,' I answered.

'Camel ride?'

'No thank you.'

Polite but assertive, I thought I'd done enough to end the conversation and go back to my dream. Not in Egypt.

'I do it cheap!'

'I don't want to ride your camel thanks.'

This was an understatement. Short of jumping out of a plane or chewing off my own arm, I couldn't think of too many things worse. The combination of awkwardly mounting a compulsive spitter, bruising my buttocks and looking like a total fool in front of strangers just didn't appeal to me. Besides, this chap was starting to get on my nerves.

'Best price sir!'

'Look, which part of NO don't you understand?'

'Ride camel at Pyramid?'

The implication that I hadn't understood the first three times was, if you'll excuse the pun, the straw that broke the camel's back. I let him have it:

'Look mate. I've got seven minutes before I have to get back on the bus. I'd rather spend my time looking at the pyramid than talking to you. I have no interest in riding your fucking camel. Got it?'

Eventually, after mumbling something under his breath, he was gone and I was left to finally appreciate the sheer scale of these amazing constructions. I was standing at the foot of something that, at four hundred and fifty feet, had been the tallest human-made structure in the world for forty-three centuries and was only eclipsed in this regard in the nineteenth century. I was comforted to learn, once boarding the bus, that our visit to the Pyramids of Giza was not yet over. We were driven to a spot that overlooked the three pyramids, and dozens of photographs were taken. Here I learned an interesting piece of information. Khafre, the son of Khufu, knew that he could not insult his father by having a larger pyramid built in his honour, so, he ordered that his slightly smaller one (by only two feet) be built on slightly higher ground. From this particular vantage point, Khafre's pyramid (the middle one) *appears* to be larger. Very clever, I thought.

It is perhaps not surprising that at a tourist haunt of such repute, I would meet my first Egyptian souvenir pedlars. I generally love bartering over souvenirs and am assertive enough to be pretty good at it. I generally start my bidding at about twenty per cent of the advertised price and only once in my life have I risen above my initial bid. Often I will walk away if the price is not coming down fast enough for my liking. I know that if they don't chase me I'm close to cost price, so I can increase my bid slightly at the next vendor. If they do chase me, I know I've got 'em. I've met some people who cannot bring themselves to bargain at all, let alone begin with such a seemingly brazen bid, either because their personality precludes it (these people often ask me to do it for them and I happily oblige), or because they think it is somehow immoral or unfair. I feel no guilt whatsoever about bringing street vendors way down in price. If they end up selling it to you—at whatever price—then they've made a profit. They're probably still ripping you off—you're just getting ripped off less severely than the gullible or overly polite buyer. It doesn't take much to see this type of tourist coming—they are often elderly, usually wearing baseball caps way up on top of their heads (I hope that doesn't give away their nationality, because I'd hate to stereotype), and tend to carry their valuables in a, shall we say, 'pickpocket-friendly' fashion. Let me share with you a few of my favourite bartering stories.

In 1997, Marina and I took a long train journey to Nice (sorry, Neetha) in the south of France. Dumping our bags in the hotel room, we sleepily descended the stairs and slumped into the restaurant across the alley. Eating our meals, we were approached by a Senegalese man selling wooden horses. These horses looked quite good, especially to Marina who had been an equestrian competitor in her teenage years, but we were in no mood to make a purchase. The woman's prerogative duly exercised, five minutes later I was ducking out into the street to see if I could find the guy and make an offer. Having no luck, I'd thought I'd try one more street and, rounding a corner, I could scarcely believe my eyes. I'd stumbled upon the pedestrian arcade, absolutely swarming with Senegalese street vendors and every single one of them selling wooden horses. After dinner, we made the purchase, discovering that the Senegalese, full of smiles and willing to plant the tongue firmly into the cheek, are great combatants in the bartering game. A lady from Sydney, whom we'd met on the train, also bought a horse and, letting our hair down, we bought a wooden, abstract *Thinker* statue. Pleased with ourselves, we sat at a café on the arcade, enjoying a beverage and admiring our purchases. It was here that we met the funniest barterer of the lot. A small Senegalese man approached, with a demeanour that reminded me of Eddie Murphy, and carrying one of the *Thinkers*. 'I'll sell you this one for forty (Francs),' he said. I replied:

'I think we've done pretty well, mate. As you can see, we've already bought three statues. Yours is beautiful too. But we're backpackers. We can only carry so many around with us.'

Missing the point (no doubt deliberately), he continued his sales pitch:

'That one no good. This one mahogany, *real* mahogany. I'll give it to you for thirty.'

He was playing the part brilliantly, but to no avail.

'This one mahogany, *real* mahogany.'

Then came the final effort. He placed the statue on the table and, moving away, said:

'Here, you take it. It's yours. Take it…'

And then, turning sharply towards us…

'…for twenty.'

I loved it—the ultimate Indian-giver. We fell about laughing. Even he laughed.

Another time I was at Badaling, on the Great Wall of China. One can only walk a few hundred metres either side of the main gate before the wall falls into various stages of disrepair. Thus, the souvenir pedlars have got you right where they want you. Walking up one side, I arrived at the end of the walking trail. I approached the last of the pedlars, inquiring about the price of a small carving (the likes of which were sold at any of a hundred places along the wall).

'Twenty (Yuan),' said the friendly man.

'I want four for ten,' I said.

'You are hard man,' said the increasingly unfriendly man. 'I've got to make living.'

'That's fine,' I said, pointing to the place next door. 'I'll buy them there.'

Realising that I could have bartered my way back to the car park, and probably cursing his place in the line, he succumbed, but not before one final effort. Handing the goods over, he baulked.

'Twelve,' he said.

'See ya!' I said.

'Ten,' he said.

I had my most bizarre bartering experience in Suva, Fiji (a place where locals will approach you, ask you your name, turn and carve the name into a wooden sword, and then apply considerable pressure on you to buy it—watch out!). Haggling over the price of a wooden phallus with a face (as you do), I finally got the price I wanted. After leaving the store, I realised that I had unwittingly walked out with a similar item under my arm, placed there while I was looking at other ones. Now I might be a 'hard man', but I'm not a dishonest one. Taking the item back to the store, I explained that I'd accidentally walked out with it but that I was now return-ing it. I loved the look on his face. He had been bowled over by my honesty. I knew he would be, and that's why I did it.

I guess after experiences such as these I can be forgiven for thinking I was qualified to pit my wits against the salesmen of Egypt. But these guys, I was soon to find out, were on a whole other level. Maybe I'm oversensitive, but I can honestly say that my experience with souvenir pedlars was one of the biggest down-ers of my trip to Egypt. What I don't like about it is that one is forced, by experience, to treat people with suspicion. These guys are very good at concealing their wares, approaching you from anywhere and getting you talking. They'll pick up on your accent—'Australian?!'—before telling you that they have a brother in Sydney. Just when you think they're a polite well-wisher, out comes the merchandise.

Once, in a Cairo backstreet, a group of us stopped to buy some chocolate. A guy was leaning on a car outside the store and, clearly well educated, started up an engaging conversation about the differences between our two countries. Two minutes later, he had his boot open trying to sell me some paintings. This sort of thing happens a lot, and it makes it very hard to take people at face value. The children you see selling mementoes at tourist sites are often far less subtle. They'll place an item on your bag or bumbag and walk briskly away, claiming that it is a 'gift'. I didn't want to find out what this meant and took to throwing the souvenir at them and making them catch it. I read in a guidebook that when asked where you are from it is a good idea to reply, 'Ya Russky'

('I am Russian'), thereby foiling their attempt to make conversation with you. Now that Russians are travelling the world in numbers, it seems these souvenir pedlars have wised up. I tried the technique once and was on the receiving end of a mouthful of Russian. I soon realised that I was never going to avoid these people. Fortunately, they are rarely permitted *inside* the main sights.

Most countries would do anything to have one or two sights as impressive as the dozens in Egypt, and on this tour we were fortunate enough to visit all of the major ones.

Arriving in Aswan by train, we spent a leisurely afternoon walking the streets, before getting some sleep in readiness for our visit to Abu Simbel. This temple, built by Ramses II in the fourteenth century BC and raised from its original spot in the 1960s during the construction of the Aswan Dam, is seemingly made for the camera. If you go to Egypt, make the effort—and it is an effort! You'll need to be up before 3.30 a.m., so that on your arrival the sun is in the right place for viewing and photos. You'll need to go by road, and you'll need to join a convoy (or, more accurately, a scene out of *The Wacky Races*). I guess there's safety in numbers— a lone vehicle would present a potential sitting duck for terrorists. If you take a minibus, it is best to take one that is not driven by the turkey we had. This guy put on an exhibition of tailgating the likes of which I'm unlikely to see again. I'd had four hours sleep, I was tired and we were travelling for three hours through a dark desert, but there was no way in the world I was going to fall asleep. Someone had to scream when we crashed. To this day, I don't understand his motives. Generally, if somebody drives an inch off another driver's rear bumper it would indicate that they feel the driver is not going fast enough and is soon to be passed. Not in this case. This fool had no inclination to pass. He just liked having no vision and being in a position where if the driver in front made the slightest error we would be dead. After one hour of this, I told Hamada to tell the prick that if he didn't pull back, I was going to ask to get out and be picked up on the way back. Thankfully it worked. But I still don't get it.

Kom Ombo and Edfu Temples were built in the Ptolemaic period (the period of Greek rule) and are impressive. I was disgusted but intrigued by the idea of early, occupying Christians methodically chiselling away just about every image of an Egyptian god or pharaoh. Strangely, they left alone the numerous erect penises that appear on the gods of fertility on temple walls throughout Egypt. Maybe they didn't want to touch them. Of course, they're not the only ones who have been guilty of this sort of barbarism over the years. With so much religious intolerance in world history, I guess we can be thankful that so many great shrines, temples, monuments and statues have remained undamaged.

Near Luxor is the Valley of the Kings. The tombs here contain such incredibly well preserved art that one is soon spoilt to the point of becoming blasé about the whole thing. Going into Tut's beautifully golden tomb (famous because it was the only one to escape tomb-raiders) was the highlight, but if you want to see his original gold mask you'll need to stop by the Egyptian Museum in Cairo.

The Temple of Queen Hatshepsut, nearby, boasts the earliest example of terracing in an Egyptian temple. Inside, one can study a detailed pictorial inventory of sacrifices and gifts made to the gods. These days, though, Hatshepsut's temple could be seen as Egypt's version of Tasmania's Port Arthur—its historical significance has been almost overshadowed by recent, sinister events. In November 1997, fifty-eight (mostly Swiss) visitors to the temple were murdered (and, in some cases, mutilated) by Islamic extremists looking to damage Egypt's government by further harming one of its main sources of income—tourism. Two months earlier, identical motives had underpinned an attack in which bullets, hand grenades and Molotov cocktails were unleashed on tourist buses outside Cairo's Egyptian Museum. On that occasion, nine were killed (including seven Germans) and nineteen were wounded. For a time the terrorists' plan worked, but relative stability in recent years has seen Egypt regain its place as a popular tourist destination. These days, though, its tourists need to become accustomed to the constant presence of machine gun-wielding police (or at least you assume they're police—some don't wear uniforms!). At first, it was undoubtedly unnerving, but after a while, it became strangely comforting. I was happy to see them—my little guardian angels watching over me. At one point, I asked Hamada what would stop an Islamic extremist joining the police ranks and then turning his gun on a bunch of tourists, especially if he were prepared to die. 'The police have all been trained,' he suggested. When I pushed the issue, I got the same response, so I gave up. But *you* understand my point, don't you?

On arriving at Karnak Temple, we were informed that the giant stone rams that adorn the entrance path originally flanked the four-kilometre road to Luxor Temple. Once I pictured this image, I was spellbound by Karnak. The place has the most massive columns I've ever seen, and I understand that the temple itself is the largest in the world. Unfortunately, Hamada had handed over the reigns to a local guide for this tour. This bloke had learned 'Guide English', memorising his mostly boring diatribe, but remaining incapable of answering any questions. I was tempted to ask who had taught him to say, 'As you can see' before every sentence. I tried not to let him bug me, and was largely success-ful. This was partly thanks to Hamada, who would turn to me and smirk or raise his eyebrows when he knew the guy had said something particularly dodgy. I was so entranced by this place that I returned that night to view the Sound and Light Show. I wish I hadn't. They basically lit up various parts of the temple in different colours and played a tape of some pontificating narrator, who perpetually 'set the scene' about the deeds of past pharaohs. I left after half an hour to watch some grass grow.

Back to Cairo and a short drive to the necropolis of Saqqara. The Step Pyramid of King Zoser is the oldest pyramid intact (about 5000 years old) and was the prototype of the three at Giza. I remember standing on the far side of the pyramid, with nobody around (except two gents trying to sell me a photo of myself), making a conscious effort to lap up the heat. I knew that after my return to England I would not experience anything like it for several months.

I did the same on what I regard as one of the highlights of the trip—a two-day Nile cruise from Aswan to Luxor (about which Top Deck's 'Essential Egypt' tour group, with whom we'd met up at a couple of points, was insanely jealous). I'm usually fairly 'sun smart' (one has to be in Australia) but all the advice I'd ever heard went out the window when I was on the upper deck of this boat. I fried myself, blaming six months in England's dismal climate for my vulnerability to flu bugs. I was convinced that the sun was doing me good. There's something about a river cruise—gently winding one's way through an ever-changing landscape. And cruising the Nile, you get to see the Egyptians and their (usually incredibly basic) living environments. Very few of them live any-where but in close proximity to this, the world's longest river.

Our cruise boat was hardly a hive of activity. Apart from us, there were fifteen passengers on board. Most were Russian or Korean and had precious little English. None was between eleven and forty years of age, so the dance floor remained desperately empty. The crew (who probably outnumbered the passengers) had very little to do, so they occupied themselves by playing tricks on us during dinner (which generally involved us ending up with water in our face or wine on our laps) and leaving little surprises for us in our rooms. The first time we went back to our room, they'd made a swan out of a towel. That's sweet, I thought. The next time they made a seductively arranged woman out of two towels with a head made out of a toilet roll and the phone attached

Stevenage: Style-free zone. Leave all ambition at the gates.

Above: Out in London. Merren and Ed are at my flanks and James is at my right ear.

Below: Me, Kevin and Mark at the Cliffs of Moher, Ireland.

Above: Milo, complete with Eurorutas bus, mullet and barracuda, Spain.

Below: With three big pointy things in Egypt.

Above: Showing off at Lake Balaton, Hungary.

Below: The Boys in Budapest—me, Mike and Turkish
—just prior to Turkish's tumble.

Above: The view from Francesco's at Ios in the Greek Islands.

Below: Friday night karaoke in Paris. Turkish, me and Vaughan.

Euro-Sterlo and Oopsi Schponkenheim at the Eiffel Tower, Paris.

Above: House, Col, me and Ron about to board
Sikker Fart, Lillehammer.

Below: With Col and House on one of several fourteen-hour
bus trips in Scandinavia. I don't know what Col is smiling about.

The Sherrin perched on a troll grave at Svartisen, Norway.

to her ear. That's a bit weird, I thought. The third time we found a full-scale imitation of a man, made chiefly of pillows, kitted out in Rafa's clothes and sporting a cap and sunglasses. At this point, we decided not to leave the room again. We thought we might return to find a horse's head in each of our beds.

On our last evening on the boat, Hamada offered to show Rafa, Hendry and me a good time in his hometown of Luxor. Things started to go awry when the boat beached itself on a sandbar in the middle of the Nile. Pretty poor form, I thought, for a craft with almost nobody on it. For us four chaps, though, the wait turned out to be a short one. Whilst they were starting to haul the boat out of the sand, Hamada—who seemed to be something of a local identity—made a call to the police, and their little vessel came to get us. In a jiffy, we were ashore at Luxor, walking along the streets and watching Hamada shoot the breeze with everyone he saw. I couldn't help noticing that things were pretty dead, a feeling confirmed by the virtual emptiness of every bar we entered. As it turned out, this particular day happened to be a fairly important religious one for Egyptian Muslims. We just couldn't take a trick that night. Still, the fact that one can freely buy alcohol in a Muslim country interests me. No doubt, the Egyptians recognise the importance of certain creature comforts for the millions of visitors whose dollars help to keep their country afloat.

Egypt's present is as disturbing as its past is awesome. Today the population is more than sixty million, the result of a sixfold increase in a century. Cairo itself is home to more than sixteen million people. Everyone seems to drive—usually dangerously, if you go by the statistics or personal observation. Air pollution levels are ten times higher than all international limits, and lower than only Mexico City. They say that being in Cairo for one day is equivalent to smoking a packet of cigarettes. A nice place to visit, but...

One of the most disturbing images for me was that of two young boys dragging their donkey through a marketplace. The animal, not surprisingly, was reluctant to move, so the boys thought it might help to slap it around the head and jump on its neck. Now I know that when in Rome and all that…but there are some actions, cultural or not, that I will not tolerate. One is pushing into a line at a shop or ticket office, and blatant cruelty is another. I approached them, quite worked up, and let fly with a barrage of crudely worded demands. Shocked, they stopped, but for how long I'll never know. I can imagine them approaching their parents later that night: 'Mum, Dad, what does "fuck" mean?'

Attempting to transcend cultural differences is often a dangerous game, as a Mandarin-speaking Australian friend of mine found out in China. Trying to tell a street vendor that it is wrong to sell tiger feet (regarded by some as an aphrodisiac), he eventually found himself being pursued by a group of fist-waving men down a hill!

While I'm on the negatives, another uncomfortable experience was our visit to a Nubian village at Aswan. The Nubians, darker-skinned, non-Arab Muslims of sub-Saharan origin, were the first inhabitants of Egypt and now form an ethnic minority group. These poor people had seen their traditional homelands flooded in 1971 with the construction of the Aswan Dam. Their village seemed desperately poor and, although foreigners were clearly appreciated for their tourist dollar, it seemed sad that they were forced to have us roaming around the buildings in which they live and work. I experienced the same phenomenon in China, where we were invited into the homes of minority peoples—I guess to see how the other half live. Again, I know they were keen to sell us stuff, but I couldn't bring myself to wander into their living rooms. I don't know if we Australians have ever done this sort of thing in Aboriginal communities, but if we have, we should be ashamed. It is a gross invasion of privacy—and cultural snobbery at its worst.

I will never forget Egypt—for reasons good and bad. I don't think my parents will ever forget my visit there either. On our final visit to Cairo, somebody in the other group referred to their parents being worried about a train disaster. 'What train disaster?' I inquired. Apparently, only two nights before, somebody on the second (or local) class train from Luxor to Cairo had decided to light a cooking fire in one of the carriages. They lost control of it and the whole train went up like a tinderbox. Hundreds were killed. I soon realised that if this was international news, and if my parents had looked at the itinerary I sent them, they might have been a touch worried. They, along with a few friends, initially unaware that the doomed train had not been first (or tourist) class, and unaware that our train from Luxor to Cairo had departed the following night, had been frantically calling government agencies requesting information. Fortunately, their fears had been allayed by the time I phoned them that night.

Not for the first time on my trip to Egypt, a country best known for the way in which it has treated its dead, I thanked my lucky stars that I was alive. If I didn't know it then, I'd know it on Monday. It was back to Slothwick.

Five
Hungary:
Attack of the Half-mongrels

In 1997, Marina and I went to Prague in the Czech Republic and promptly fell in love with the place. It really is the most gorgeous of cities—compact, beautifully preserved (though I have since read criticisms of the pastel paint jobs, allegedly unfaithful to the original look of the city) and reminiscent of a fairytale world. Besides, it is (or at least was in 1997) dirt cheap…laughably cheap. I remember us being in a pub one day and getting two one-litre glasses of beer and two meatloaves for less than five Aussie dollars. This sort of thing, I have found, inevitably improves one's mood. Whilst raving about Prague to fellow travellers I had been told that I should also check out Budapest. It was, according to my informants, just as pretty as Prague, less touristy and even cheaper. Furthermore, you could get to Budapest from Vienna via a seven-hour hydrofoil ride, which sounded like a suitably romantic way to arrive in a place. Knowing that I wouldn't have time in that year, I made a note in my little black book. Another time…

I knew in March/April 2002, when the spring holidays rolled around, that I would be making my way to Budapest. I considered hitting Prague again on the same trip for old times' sake, but eventually decided that I wanted to see as much of Hungary as I could in the ten days. The hydrofoil thing was still an option, until I found out that it didn't start until mid-April—I was going to miss it by a few days. So, the plan became a simple one: fly into Budapest, stay until I got bored, visit some other parts of Hungary, return to Budapest and fly home. I felt as though I could use a couple of partners-in-crime for this adventure, so a few weeks before departure I started to work on my two mates and work colleagues, Mike and Richard.

Mike, as it turned out, didn't require too much convincing. 'Lock me in!' he said almost immediately, keen to give a test-run to the Australian expression he had picked up from his new 'convict' mate. Mike is a short, sporty PE teacher in his mid-twenties who works at Slothwick Skool. He was (and still is, no doubt) a binge-drinking phenomenon with a sharp, cheeky wit. Every Monday he would slink into work, his eyes bloodshot and his hands shaking, desperately trying to hydrate himself. By lunchtime, he had usually recovered to the point at which he would regale us with stories from his weekend. Friday night he would usually get drunk. Saturday morning he would play football (soccer) and get sent off for a two-footed challenge or telling the ref to 'Get fucked!' (or sometimes both). Saturday night he would start drinking at 'The Oak' (in Welwyn Garden City) before adjourning to 'The Squash [Club]' and trying to have his wicked way with any girl who was willing, getting thoroughly pissed all the while. Sunday, he would play twenty minutes of football before vomiting on the pitch and being replaced. And on Sunday afternoon, 'the best drink of the week', he would get stuck into it again, to the point where he would inevitably need to go to bed at 3.30 on a Monday afternoon after barely making it through the day.

My favourite Mike story is this one. He and his friends met at noon one Saturday in London to 'do the Circle Line'. For those of you unacquainted with the London Underground, the Circle Line is the track that winds a circular path around inner London. It has twenty-eight stops. At each of these stops, the boys were bound to get off the train, find the nearest pub and drink a pint or a shot. After quite a number of stops on this particular day, Mike fell asleep on the train and, unbeknownst to him, had his shoelaces tied together by one of his buddies. The train stopped, people got off, and just when the siren began to indicate that the doors were about to close, the boys shook Mike awake. He stood, tried to run and promptly fell flat on his face. Here's what impressed me. At that moment, drunk, groggy and undoubtedly in pain, Mike had the presence of mind to reach out with his hands, grab the threshold of the train doorway as the doors were closing and propel himself on his stomach on to the platform. The visuals get me every time. He must have looked like a seal at Sea World arriving on the pontoon for a fishy treat.

The second guy I targeted, Richard, generally needs convincing to walk to the end of his street. To my surprise, he signed up after only a few days of me saying, 'Come on, come on, come on...' A science teacher just the other side of thirty, Richard is a vastly different character to Mike. Defiantly Welsh, though born in England (he'll hate me writing that), Richard is a tall, humble, quiet and fairly unadventurous guy—at least until he gets on the booze. He insists, despite regular coaching, on breaking world speed records with his first few drinks. This leads to him being the life of the party for about fifteen minutes before he inevitably falls asleep—always before 10.00 p.m. and often face-first in a curry. I've never seen anything like it in my life. But Richard, like Mike, is unfailingly loyal and has a heart of gold. I'm proud to call both of them my friends.

Neither man had travelled a great deal outside of the UK, and some of my colleagues thought I had my work cut out. 'You're going to take those two around Hungary!' they would say, barely concealing their glee at the prospect. It was as if I was about to lead a school trip, consisting of a couple of 'students at risk'. It was a win-win situation really—they were happy to be led and I'm always happiest leading. I must admit, though, that I didn't expect my fun to start at London's Heathrow Airport. The fact that Richard had never flown before, along with his tendency to be rather gullible, saw Mike and I preparing him for all sorts of bizarre situations on the plane. I've never seen Richard drink a pint so slowly. As it turned out, he handled the flight to Vienna without any problems. When he saw our little twenty-seater, however, with its propellers churning in readiness for the flight to the Hungarian capital, he lost a fair bit of his composure. I don't think he spoke until after we landed.

Arriving at Budapest Airport, we met Joe, the provider of our accommodation for the first three nights. When I had booked the apartment over the phone several weeks before, Joe had offered to drive out to the airport to pick us up. I thought at the time that this was remarkably generous, but when I realised that it was a fifty-minute drive I was ready to declare the guy a saint. He spoke English well and was a happy, affable sort of chap. He was keen to point out sites of interest on the way, going to great pains to show us the Burger King in the centre of town—'the biggest in Europe' he exclaimed with pride. We found this hilarious and couldn't wait to get up there and have photos taken of us raising our index finger skyward. Number one—and we were actually there!

We arrived at our lodgings to find them spartan (as they often are in Eastern Europe), but adequate. Joe sat down with a map and helped us to get our bearings. He then asked us for the money to cover the three nights (a pittance) and we obliged, including a healthy tip (or a small one if you converted to pounds) for all of his assistance. At this point, he was clearly moved by what he perceived as our generosity and he began to cry. This was our first meeting with a Hungarian and we were touched.

Throughout our trip, we found the Hungarian people, almost without exception, to be honest, helpful, tolerant and amiable. Budapest in particular is an extremely cosmopolitan place, and Hungarians seem to be relishing their place in the new, post-Cold War Europe. They are a proud people, but determined to adopt new ideas. This is summed up in the attitude of a Hungarian exchange student whom I recently taught in Canberra. He travelled across the globe to learn our language, our history and the techniques of our best water polo coaches. Yet, he is so proud of being Hungarian that his eyes lit up when I mentioned the place.

For dinner on that first night, Joe suggested we try a restaurant fifty metres up the road. 'Simon's', he told us, offered traditional Hungarian fare and wasn't about to put a dent in the wallet. He wasn't wrong. The food was outstanding—goulash, goose leg, wild boar, pancakes 'hortobagy style' (whatever that means) and a delightful creamy dessert for which the translation was 'Or wie have or wie don't have'. We learned not to ask questions—we just ate…and ate…and ate. It was amusing to watch Richard trying to exercise some self-control with all this beautiful food around. 'I'm full,' he would say. 'Couldn't possibly fit another thing in.' Within seconds, he'd be going in for one more mouthful…then another…and another. We started to test him after a while, putting little morsels of our food on his empty plate and pushing it towards him. He'd invariably take the bait. I thought *I* loved food—this guy is incredible!

After dinner we went for a walk, and promptly discovered that the women of Budapest are absolutely gorgeous—right up there with Scandinavian and Spanish girls. That set the tone for ten days of the three of us wandering around like rubbernecks. Physiotherapy was required on return.

On our second day, we hit the streets for a long day of sightseeing. The Danube, particularly full during our visit, divides the castle district of Buda and the flat commercial region of Pest. (The city was originally called Pest-Buda.) Several bridges join the two—the most distinctive being Chain Bridge. Architecturally, the whole city is a treat, but for me the highlight was undoubtedly the Parliament Building which graces the riverbank on the Pest side. Neo-Gothic in design, this gem was built by the same team that produced the Parliament Building at Westminster. It was completed in 1904, but we three laymen agreed that it looked considerably older than that. Climbing through Buda to the Royal

Palace and Fisherman's Bastion brought the opportunity for some fabulous photographs of this grand city—the 'Paris of the East'. The descent gave us our first 'Turkish' story.

Richard didn't earn the name 'Turkish' until we had left Budapest, but it seems strange now to refer to him as anything else. If you're looking for a crazy story about the inception of this nickname, you will be sorely disappointed. Mike had, for several days, been quoting lines from *Snatch*, one of his favourite films. These lines included the now immortal: 'Put a leash on him Turkish, or he'll get hurt' (which, of course, had more appeal when spoken in Mike's cockney accent). One day, in Pécs (pronounced 'Pairch'—a pretty town a couple of hours south of Budapest), Richard decided to take on the job of purchasing some rail tickets, while Mike and I checked our emails at an Internet café. When we finished, we stood in the street waiting for what seemed an eternity. 'Where's Turkish?' Mike asked rhetorically, looking left, then right. Seconds later, at the bottom of the street, Richard appeared. By the time I said, 'There's Turkish', you may as well have started engraving the bloke's headstone. Now everyone I know calls him Turkish, and he has absolutely no say in it. Later, we were to learn that the inhabitants of Turkish's hometown Llanelli (don't bother trying to pronounce it unless you're Welsh) are known as 'Turks' by their rivals in nearby Swansea. It seems it was meant to be.

If Hollywood ever makes a movie based on our trip to Hungary (unlikely, I admit), the producers will need to find a slapstick genius to do justice to Turkish. The path that leads up to the landmarks of Buda is a winding one—zigzagging its way up the hill. Coming back down, Mike and I didn't have the patience to wander back and forth across the slope. We thought we'd just skip straight down the hill on the grass, pausing as we came to each section of the paved path. Turkish, whose accident-prone nature had been more or less kept hidden up to this point, was sceptical of the plan, but was persuaded to negotiate the first challenge—a five-metre grassy slope to the next piece of the path. Emboldened, he thought he'd try the second section—closer to ten metres in length. It was hardly elegant but a success nonetheless. The third and final section was to the bottom of the hill—a distance of around forty metres and very steep. I think we only attempted it because we could sense that Turkish thought we wouldn't. Mike and I chose different routes, each progressing in a sideways fashion and each pausing regularly so as not to build up too much momentum and lose control. It was during one of these pauses that I sensed something approaching me, with alarming velocity, from behind. I turned just in time to avoid Turkish's outstretched arms—matador-style—as the big monster tried to grab me on the way through. I knew that if he had gotten hold of me, I would have gone with him. The distance from where we were to the bottom was great enough for Mike and me to stand for several seconds and watch the results of this unintended stunt. By the time Turkish neared the bottom he was fully sprinting but, as the path approached, I was still confident that he might be able to level out and stay on his feet. How wrong I was. As he hit the path, the abrupt change of angle saw him lose his balance. He toppled forward and ploughed shoulder-first into the dirt on the other side. Reaching for my first aid kit, I discovered my camera and was able to capture the aftermath on film.

As the trip progressed, Mike and I were treated to many more of these special Turkish moments. One day he bought a hamburger, walked outside, went for his first bite, and dropped the thing all over the ground in front of a dozen people. (I must stress, though, that it wasn't his fault, but that of the substandard packaging.) Another day while we were walking along, a sign approached, Turkish forgot to duck, and down he went. The two of us tried our best to make him more street-smart, deliberately crossing at the most hazardous sections of four-lane roads just to get him used to it. But nothing seemed to work.

On Day Three, Turkish lost his credit card and needed to borrow cash for the remainder of the trip. We began to trial other nicknames for him, such as 'Calamity Rich' or 'The Weakest Link', but invariably came back to 'Turkish'. On a weekender to Paris in the following June with a group of Slothwick teachers (a trip which forms the basis for Chapter Seven), dinner was booked at a tasteful, provincial restaurant in the Montmartre district. Turkish drank a bottle of red in five minutes, became loud and overly affectionate, fell dangerously close to a cabinet full of crystal, was carried outside where he hugged everyone in sight including passers-by, finally got into a taxi (the first one refused to stop) and was put to bed by two of our party. And all this before 10.00 p.m.! At 3.00 a.m., when the same two guys returned to the hotel, they stopped by his room to check on him. He was gone. Thirty minutes later he returned to the room, was asked a few questions, did his best Marcel Marceau impression (mouth closed, hands out, palms upturned), and then collapsed. The marks on his wrists indicated that he had been mugged—apparently inside the hotel! His watch had disappeared, as had his wallet, including (you guessed it) his new credit card. Turkish rarely had a big night out without waking the next day to find on his body a selection of cuts, bruises and scars, the causes of which were of course a complete mystery to him. And I think he is now on first name terms with the guy on the Lost Credit Card Hotline.

The nightlife of Budapest is held in high regard. Unfortunately, we arrived just prior to peak season, but there was enough going on to keep us interested. On our first night out, we encountered a table full of girls who, it soon became clear, were English.

'Which part of England are you from?' we enquired.

'Hertfordshire,' one of them replied.

'Really? Us too. Whereabouts?'

'Stevenage.'

Shit! I'd flown across Europe to escape the stinking place. I looked around to see if any of my students had tracked me down.

Another night I danced with a girl who was, according to an inebriated and totally irrational Turkish, his girlfriend. (Apparently, speaking more than two sentences to a girl earns you boyfriend status.) Later, choosing to walk back to our accommodation instead of joining Mike and Turkish in a four hundred-metre taxi ride, I stopped off for a slice of traditional Hungarian pizza. Arriving minutes later, I found them sitting on the doorstep, unable to get in because I had the only key. Turkish jumped to his feet, berated me for stealing his girlfriend or wife or whatever she was, and started hurling an empty water bottle at me. The exertion was all too much for him, and pretty soon he fell over. The next morning, aware that Turkish's 'morning after' memory leaves a lot to be desired, I thought I'd see how gullible he was. Winking at Mike, I pretended I was angry with Turkish and asked him how his head was.

'It's okay. Why?' he asked.

'Can't you remember what happened last night?'

'No. What?'

'You wanted a shot at my title. You wanted to take me on.'

'I did not!'

'You did. You played with fire and you got burned.'

I then 're-enacted' a scene in which he had thrown a water bottle at me, I had remonstrated with him, he had thrown a punch and I had been forced to head-butt him (as if I'd even know how). I was at pains to point out that he shouldn't mess with somebody who happened to be 'in a purple patch' and 'at the peak of his powers'. It was a genuine cliché-fest. Mike, with some help from a pillow, did a sterling job in keeping a straight face. This was despite the fact that I claimed he had gotten into the act by propelling himself from his bed and fly-kicking Turkish in the guts. After Turkish apologised to us for acting in this manner, we let him in on the ruse. Maybe it's the child in me, but I love that sort of stuff. It served Turkish right, really, for being such a prat.

Have you heard enough about Turkish yet? Just let me tell you about this little paranoia that he had. Both of my travelling companions were keen to have a read of my *Lonely Planet* guidebook at down times. It's called *Europe on a Shoestring*, and it contains chapters on forty countries. Being from Wales, and somewhat overprotective of it, Turkish turned to the Wales section to see what the authors thought of his little part of the world. He was unimpressed to the point where he quickly became too worked up to read it properly. At one point the book says:

'[Wales] sometimes feels rather like England's unloved back yard—a suitable place for coal mines and nuclear power stations.'

Now I read that as a comment on the exploitation of Wales by its colonising, dominating neighbour. Turkish thought the authors of the book were saying that Wales *was* only suitable for coal mines and nuclear power stations. He launched a tirade on the book's authors, its publishers, its readers, their parents and anyone they had ever known. I tried to placate him by suggesting that he look at some of the other chapters in the book—perhaps the reports on other countries were less than glowing.

'Try Romania,' I said, 'and Bulgaria'.

Each time he was deflated even further. They were all more positive than the section on Wales. At this point, we should have let it drop, but what fun are mates if you can't get them going—especially Turkish. Mike, half-Welsh himself, started the ball rolling.

'Tell us what is worth seeing in Wales, Turkish. What does it have besides slag pits, rubbish dumps and sewage works?'

'It's got beaches. There are some beautiful beaches in Wales.'

'Yeah,' I piped up. 'But if you're after beaches you'd go to Hawaii…or South Africa…or Australia.'

'It's got castles.'

'Yeah but…'

And so on…for the rest of the afternoon. Eventually he pulled out his trump card. 'We've got druids!' We couldn't keep it together when we heard this one. Even now, when Turkish talks of visiting me in Australia, he says he'll only do it if I can promise him druids. 'Any destination worth its salt has druids,' he claims.

The next four stories involve bums, boobs and/or genitals. You've been warned.

Mike, a sports nut, had never been to a museum in his life. I'd threatened to take him to one for weeks and I figured that the National Museum of Hungary in Budapest was as good a place as any. As it happens, I was soon finding this museum a little on the boring side, but I was heartened to observe Mike staring intently in the direction of one of the exhibits.

'What is it?' I asked, looking more closely at a glass cabinet full of weapons.

'Have a look at her arse,' he said, motioning to a nearby patron.

I refused to give up on the idea of getting some Hungarian culture into us. One day I announced that we should check out the thermal baths—that was something distinctively Hungarian. The boys agreed that it was worth a go, so we headed off to Budapest's Szechenyi Baths. After twenty minutes working out how much we should pay, we entered and found the experience most satisfactory. We loved the challenge of sticking it out in the world's hottest sauna (at least that's where we rated it) and found the various pools, with their differing temperatures, incredibly relaxing. After our visits to the towns of Pécs and Balatonfured (a tourist haunt on Lake Balaton, Europe's largest lake outside of Scandinavia), we returned to our beloved Budapest and decided to sample the famous Gellert Baths. Here, as at Szechenyi, some sections are mixed and it is just like hanging out at one's local swimming pool. Other areas at Gellert, however, are single sex only and have a decidedly gay feel. Either that or Hungarian brothers are very close. At one point, in the sauna, it came to my attention that one gentleman, attired in his birthday suit, had become slightly aroused. I knew that Mike had seen it too. Knowing that it was unlikely that those present spoke English let alone Australian profano-slang, I felt comfortable in sharing my find with Mike and Turkish. 'That bloke's got a half-mongrel,' I announced. Just quietly, 'half' was being a little conservative. It was enough to prompt a speedy change of rooms.

One night in Pécs (aptly named, as you'll soon see) we were won over by a brilliant marketing strategy—well, brilliant if your market happens to be a triumvirate of desperate deviants like us. Entering a bar, we ordered three Stella Artois (the Belgian and now all-conquering lager) and, curiously, were given three tickets. We didn't know what the tickets were for, but we were soon approached by three absolute stunners wearing Stella Artois t-shirts. The girls said something in Magyar (Hungary-speak) but soon realised we were aliens. One then spoke English to me: 'Please choose one of us girls.' I had never known girls to work so fast. 'What do you mean?' I replied. 'Come here,' she said, leading me by the arm behind a nearby screen. She then removed her t-shirt to reveal two breasts barely covered by a tiny bra. Apparently (as I can't remember, being quite taken aback by the experience), my response to this was to utter the compliment: 'Very nice.' At this point, the girl gave me the shirt and put on a new one. We were so shocked by this that we became very thirsty, and it's funny, but only Stella Artois seemed to truly quench our thirst that night. Anyone need a t-shirt?

We were very proud with the little joke we came up with a couple of beers down the track. When it was Mike's turn to choose a girl, all three lined up before him. I stood next to them, proudly wearing my Stella t-shirt. Mike then did the eeny-meeny-miney-mo thing, before pointing at me. I started to remove my t-shirt and…eventually they understood the joke.

Many of you have no doubt marvelled at the badgering skills and sheer persistence of strip show touts and pimps—at Kings Cross in Sydney if nowhere else. One night I hit the sack early and the boys came back with a story of a sales pitch that puts all others to shame. Here is a transcript:

'Hey boys! This is [with great emphasis] fucking good shit! Spanky wanky, bondage, domination, top notch pussy! Big tits—no silicone!'

'We're off. Maybe later.'

'NOW, not later! The girls will go to sleep and you'll get no sucky sucky, no fucky fucky and you'll have to go home and spank the monkey!'

'Maybe later.'

'Okay, but if you change your mind, my name is Marius.'

An offer too good to refuse, and yet they did. I'm proud of you, lads.

One of the greatest legacies of my time in Hungary was the appreciation I gained for the 'Euroboy'. For the uneducated, (and this is the first time I've attempted to define this type of individual, so bear with me) a Euroboy is a young man from any continental European country who speaks English, has adopted British and American culture, music and lingo, and is about ten years behind the times but thinks he's at the cutting edge of cool. He will often sport a mullet hairstyle, and set it off with a collection of fashion items that would be more at home in the wardrobes of Duran Duran. One night, walking around in pre-peak season Balatonfured, wishing we were there two months later, we heard sounds in the distance that suggested that the entire town might not be dead. As we got closer—no word of a lie—we could hear young men shouting, 'Party, party, Eurostyle!' in thick German accents. This had a great impact on me, and would eventually lead to the creation of a character of mine, but for now I was happy to join the party at a two-tiered club and add my own voice to the cacophony.

'Party, party, party! Sexy, sexy, sexy!'

There aren't too many places in the world where it is acceptable, nay expected, for one to carry on with this sort of rot. It seems I had finally found the promised land.

Six
The Greek Isles:
Oopsi Did It Again!

I'd been to Greece before, spending time in Athens, Delphi and the spectacular island of Santorini. Some countries you see and enjoy, but never feel the urge to return. For me, Greece is not one of those countries. I can see myself going to Greece again and again, finances permitting. The colours are superb—white, simple houses set against deep blue seas and rocky hills and outcrops. The food is reliably good—meat lovers will be well satisfied, whilst vegetarians can delight in the omelettes, vegie moussaka, stuffed vine leaves and, of course, Greek salads. Greece is still relatively inexpensive, though how long this will last I don't know. The weather is rarely anything less than perfect, and this seems to have produced a generally happy, relaxed population. At the June half-term break, I was looking for a place to unwind before cutting loose. I chose well.

High season approaching, I thought it wise to book some accommodation before I left. (As it turns out, I needn't have bothered—there are always places to stay on the islands.) My plan was to arrive in Athens, make my way immediately to the nearby port of Piraeus, catch a ferry to Naxos, and, three days later, make my way to Ios.

Naxos is the largest island in the group known as the Cyclades. Forty kilometres across, it offers much to those willing to hop on a moped. On my first night in Hora (Naxos Town), I met a great girl from New York called Mara. She too had just arrived on the island and seemed keen to have a look around. The next day we hired mopeds for a very reasonable price and helmets to go with them. Any plans one has of looking chic quickly evaporate when one of these massive cranial appendages is donned. Furthermore, imagine a really bad case of 'hat hair', triple it, and you've got 'helmet hair'. But, given the high rate of fatalities on Greek roads (a fact supported by the profusion of roadside memorials), it is an unavoidable inconvenience.

Mara and I spent a fantastic day traversing the island. We saw the elevated town of Filoti, the highest peak of Mt Zeus (1001m) including a visit to The Cave of Zeus (a.k.a. The Cave of Goat Shit), and the quieter than quiet resort town of Moutsouna on the east coast. Here, as I looked back at the huge mountain we had just descended, the frightening possibility of running out of fuel hit me for the first time. It's amazing how economically you can drive (or, in this case, ride) when you really try, and this time I got away with it. One thing that interests me about Greece is the number of unfinished buildings one sees. It is as though they run out of money or energy and will return in ten or twenty years when they have found a little of either. Back at Hora, the Temple of Apollo that juts out into the harbour, also seemingly unfinished, presents a top photo opportunity, particularly at sunset. I spent the following day relaxing on the beach and my batteries were sufficiently recharged to tackle nearby Ios.

Some people will tell you that Ios is actually an acronym for 'Island of Sleeze'. Having spent four days there, I can see why they would say that. It is an island that seems to exist for the sole purpose of partying.

One arrives at the port and, unless over forty, doesn't return until ready to leave the island. Youngsters head straight for the village, at the highest point of the island. I stayed at a place in the village called Francesco's, which really is something of an institution. Overlooking the harbour, it offers a bar at which travellers ritually meet every night at about 9.00 p.m. before hitting the clubs. The itinerary for a summer day at Ios never varies:

12 noon: Wake up

12.30 p.m.: Breakfast, usually an omelette

1.30 p.m.: Pay 80 (Euro) cents to catch a bus over the hill and down to Mylopotas Beach, at the far end of which is Far Out Camping

2.00 p.m.–7.00 p.m.: Swim in the pool at Far Out, drink beers, eat food, and rubberneck it

7.30 p.m.: Shower and change at hotel

8.00 p.m.: Eat

9.00 p.m.: Drinks (at Francesco's for many)

10.30 p.m.–dawn: Party VERY hard—Eurostyle if you dare

Most debauchery takes place in the village square. When looking for the square by day, don't blink or you'll miss it. (I did the first time.) Apparently, at the height of summer, it is near impossible to cross due to the enormous swathe of bodies. The square is surrounded by a labyrinth of little alleys, each containing bars which are all very similar. It's hard to remember the names. I can recall the Slammer Bar, because of the barmaid, and the Red Bull Bar, because it was here that I was kissed on the cheek by several large, bristly Englishmen who appreciated the fact that I was wearing an English football (soccer) shirt on the night of their famous World Cup victory over Argentina.

I made numerous friends in my time on Ios, and by telling you something about each of them, you'll learn a little about my wild time on this positively nutty island.

I'm not sure that I'd call Oopsi my friend, but he probably left a more indelible impression on me than anybody. On the night I met Mara in a bar on Naxos, the two of us watched with a healthy mix of awe and pity as this German Euroboy extraordinaire danced and flirted wildly with a Danish woman resembling Brigitte Nielsen. This woman's body was so muscular that I'm sure she could have cracked walnuts between her butt-cheeks, if requested. At one point, the guy got a real shock when, presumably to demonstrate her athletic prowess and enviable flexibility, Brigitte lent back and delivered a swift kick up the front of his face. While we, along with our friendly, intoxicated and increasingly generous barman Adonis (I know it's starting to sound fabricated but I swear it isn't) were wetting ourselves with laughter, I'm sure the Euroboy was doing the same with fear. Later, he was keen to talk to us about his ordeal. I asked him to say and then spell his name several times, and I can confirm that his name was indeed Oopsi.

From that moment, Oopsi and his brother/mate/lover (I've no idea) Mike (who, like Oopsi, bore a disturbing resemblance to Canadian rocker Bryan Adams) kept turning up everywhere, no matter what island I was on. I saw him several times on Naxos in the next forty-eight hours and I lost count of how many times he crossed my path in Ios. Each time I saw him I would exclaim 'Oopsi!', and handshakes would ensue. Inevitably, I would mention the infamous kick and each time he would re-enact it. On my second night in Ios, I met an Aussie tour guide called Glenn (whose group comprised one person, and she liked to get twelve hours sleep every day, thereby officially making his the world's easiest job). Before going out on the town, I filled Glenn in on the Oopsi highlights and predicted that we would see Oopsi within an hour. Five minutes after leaving Francesco's I let out a cry of 'Oopsi!' He was there in the square, with Mike in tow, and he was soon making a hammy-crunching attempt to recreate the kick for us. Introductions made, we went our separate ways, but we saw him several more times that evening. Glenn and I parted later in the night, and at breakfast the next day he recounted how he had managed to end up on hugging terms with Oopsi by dawn. Now there's something for the CV!

One night I went to bed relatively early. Glenn and a few of the other blokes went out and were sorry to report that they hadn't seen Oopsi at all. I was shocked:

'You're kidding! I saw him four times without leaving my room. Once he poked his head in the window, another time he was in the wardrobe…'

I was joking of course. Perhaps he had left the island. On my last day at Ios, at Far Out Camping, an appalling band started their set with the Britney Spears tune 'Oops!...I did it again', which of course became 'Oopsi did it again'. He may not have been there in body, but he was there in spirit.

I met Ben, a twenty-one year old Canadian, on the ferry across to Ios. Young and brash, he kept telling me how he'd learned to drink at college and how he could handle his liquor. I must admit, he could put the stuff away. Hitting it hard on the first night, he eventually tried to stumble home before passing out in one of the alleys. An American guy—a complete stranger—came along, somehow got some sense out of him and was able to help him to his door. Without a key, Ben slumped on the door mat. This good samaritan later told us that when he had returned to the village square a short time later, there was Ben with a beer in his hand. Inexplicably, Ben had beaten him back to the square. The sign, I guess, of a true drinker—the ability to rise above unconsciousness.

Joe and Ben (another Ben) are two American guys whom I met at Francesco's on the first day. With a group now comprising a Joe, two Bens and two Glenns, it seemed a shame not to start up a boy band. Our first lip-sync show, in the Slammer Bar, had mixed reviews. But with Joe comin' in from da west and Ben One from da east, me getting down and dirty, and Ben Two and Glenn just dudin' it free-form, we were surprised that we remained in obscurity. Actually, we weren't all that surprised.

Also on the first day I met two New Yorkers, Nick and Brad. They were nice guys—just out of their minds. That first afternoon, both blokes drank like they had just been let out of gaol or something. Rarely have I seen guys stand around a pool with a screwdriver (vodka and orange, as we Aussies call it) in each hand.

Soon they were off the radar. Word had it that they had been seen skinny-dipping with a bunch of girls at ten the next morning. Absolutely trashed, they went AWOL for two days.

On the third night, we all met up again and swapped a few stories. I sensed by the way Nick and Brad were putting away the drinks that they were in for another bender, and that we wouldn't be seeing much of them. As it turns out, they persuaded a moped hire place to rent them two of their machines for the night. (This in itself was an effort because in Ios, unlike Naxos, they usually demand to see a motorcycle licence.) After an all-night drinking session, they were riding their mopeds at 6.00 a.m. when Nick, about six feet six inches tall, lost control and crashed head-on into a taxi. He, like Bill Cosby's cartoon superhero 'The Brown Hornet', miraculously escaped unharmed. The bike, the taxi and his finances did not. Brad witnessed the accident but, inexplicably paranoid and convinced that he would be going to the 'big house', checked that his friend was alive and fled into the hills. As he told me the next afternoon at the hotel, he then fell asleep on a mountainside and woke some time later, in broad daylight, surrounded by a herd of goats and their shepherd. I listened in disbelief to these tales but must have expressed enough interest for Brad to tell me a story from his college days. I include the story here, begging you to understand that I do not condone the actions of these men in any of these tales. It's just that I find their knack of finding trouble very comical.

Brad, I should tell you, is Sylvester Stallone. No, I don't mean he talks like Stallone or looks like Stallone or acts like Stallone. I mean he actually is Stallone. Well I could never tell the difference. So, picture Stallone, leaning back in a chair, feeling sorry for himself, and telling this story:

'So here I was with a bunch of my frat buddies in the back of a rented utility. We each drank a case of Bud in an orchard. Then I was doin' burnouts in the truck—donuts and all kindsa crazy shit. I blew a fuckin' tyre and then busted the rim. So I started jumpin' on the hood, shouting "I've got insurance! I've got insurance!" The boys got in the car and we started to make our way back to the camp site, drivin' on the rim. We decided to make up this story that the truck was trashed 'cause we hit a deer. Then on the side of the road, we saw a dead deer. I had this idea… Five minutes later a policeman came along to find me sitting next to the truck, holding my knife in one hand and a deer's leg in the other! Man, some of these guys I was with were friggin' vegans and I had them smearin' deer blood on the truck. I thought to myself: How am I gonna get out of this one? I said to the cop: "Look officer, these things happen. Hey, you're a white guy, I'm a white guy. What say we forget all about this?"'

Brad told me that he thought he should hurry up and start a family so he'd be forced to stop doing stuff like this. I guess there's some logic in that. You may or may not be surprised to know that both Nick and Brad were about to commence a career in investment banking in the Big Apple. I hope they get themselves good lawyers…and good undertakers.

Seven
'I Like to Party!':
Peace and Deep Beatz
on the Streetz of Paris

'The Tour' had been keenly awaited. Sixteen teachers, wound up like coiled springs from months of waging war in the classroom, were about to launch themselves on the French capital. And if Paris had any innocence left to lose, this was the weekend when it would finally be stripped away.

I had been to Paris before and had seen most of the major sights. I'm not saying there was nothing more for me to do there (as one could clearly explore it for months without becoming bored), but as far as I was concerned, the pressure to be a tourist was off. On this June weekend, I went in search of a mighty two-day bender, and I certainly found it.

Some of my best mates were on the tour—Turkish and Mike (whom you know from my Budapest adventures), Vaughan (whom I mentioned was my immediate boss), Rick (who drove Turkish and me to work every day), Jon (Head of English, tour organiser and very funny guy), and Jude (the Aussie girlfriend of my flatmate Kev). The one person I need to make special mention of is Vic, a twenty-eight year old English teacher who turned out to be my partner-in-crime on this trip.

Vic had been at Slothwick for a year before I arrived. She and I were incompatible in some ways, but shared very similar senses of humour. I think the only time I laughed and she didn't was the time Mike pinned a pair of her knickers (the manner of their capture escapes me) to the staffroom noticeboard, and it took her a full day to discover them. In Paris, Vic and I decided (for a laugh) to have a competition to see how many times we could 'cop off' with the locals. To 'cop off' is basically to kiss somebody for an extended period. (I think it might derive from the verb 'to copulate' but it generally does not involve sex.) It is a fantastic term and, to the consternation of my Australian friends, it is irremovably etched into my vocabulary. It is beautifully harsh— like you (the 'copper') are meting out some sort of punishment on the hapless 'copee'.

Can you imagine a circumstance in which a passable looking fellow could convince more people to kiss him than could an attractive looking girl? With the grand total of zero, I was slaughtered. What made it memorable, however, was the accompanying banter between the two of us. In a nightclub, Vic would kiss a guy, turn to me and say, 'Look, I'm copping off', and go in for more. We were 'on the cop' for two days. Because I wasn't getting any (I'll blame the language barrier…and the fact that the French hate the Poms and no doubt thought I was one), I tried to introduce a system whereby one could score fractions of cops. If a member of the opposite sex looked at you, you earned a quarter cop. If they touched you, that was a half cop. I wished I'd never introduced this rule when the two of us were in the backseat of a taxi, a car drove past, and Vic claimed: 'I've just copped off!' Apparently, the four guys in the car had looked at her. Vic left Slothwick at the same time I did, and in her leaving speech she thanked the people on staff with whom she had copped off (there were a couple), as well as apologising to all those who wanted to cop off with her but were unable—and then she named them.

I slept for a total of four hours over two nights in Paris. We were pissed on the Eurostar on the way over, more pissed at the karaoke bar in Paris, and too tired to be pissed when we (well, four of us) stumbled into bed at 6.00 a.m. The next day, after two hours sleep, we were drinking beer with brunch. At midday, we had arranged to meet the majority of the group at the Eiffel Tower. It was here that I introduced the world to Oopsi Schponkenheim.

The tour group was hardly a conservative one, though they did go to galleries and a church on that Saturday morning, and they did think that being crazy meant coordinating the wearing of Hawaiian shirts on the train. Regarding this as a fraction tame, I thought I'd go a couple of steps further and invent an alter ego.

Oopsi Schponkenheim is a character based partly on the hilarious Oopsi of Naxos and Ios, and partly on the archetypal Euroboy, dozens of whom I had recently met in Hungary. When I was in Greece, I purchased a thoroughly ridiculous 'muscle shirt' which was predominantly black with pink lightning bolts shooting across it. I bought a similar one for Mike, whom I knew would be into it. His was purple with white tie-dye stripes. To these garments, we added thick pseudo-gold medallions on thick quasi-gold chains and, of course, our wigs. Mike's started as a basic blonde wig before we took the scissors to it. (While one fillets a fish, one 'mullets' a wig.) We attacked the sides with gusto until we had produced a look that I termed (for rugby league fans) 'Euro-Sterlo'. My wig was brown and, as has been mentioned in an earlier chapter, had already been fashioned into a cracking mullet—short at the sides, spiky on top and nice and long at the back. Now we were ready to make our presence felt in the city of love.

None amongst the tour group knew about our planned Euroboy stunt, and I think they were somewhat taken aback when Oopsi and friend rolled up to the famous tower and gleefully announced: 'There's a party in my pants...and everybody's invited!' Perhaps at this point I should attempt to explain the rationale behind my character Oopsi.

Oopsi basically goes around saying stuff, generally at the top of his voice. His accent is European—and that's as specific as I can be. There are a number of key elements that make up his personality, and I set these out below:

1. *He assumes that everybody needs to know exactly what he thinks.* Examples of this are the standard 'I like sex' or 'It's funny, but I like to schponk', usually followed up with 'Oh, but it's very nice', regardless of whether there has been an objection or not. Comments like this are inserted where they are least expected or appropriate, for maximum effect. It is always as if somebody has asked his opinion on something, when they haven't.

2. *He states the obvious, as if nobody has ever thought of it before.* This tendency is probably best illustrated by the call 'beer is nice' or 'women make me happy'. He is clearly no radical, though he does stop short of saying, 'Oxygen is nice'.

3. *He is unfailingly positive.* Everything is 'wonderful', 'very nice', 'sexy' or occasionally even 'bitching'.

4. *He announces things with a sense of foreboding, as if the whole damn world had better look out.* Frequently, he will admit to being 'horny!' or that things are making him 'hard!' It's a warning to those around him more than anything else.

5. *He loves himself to death.* Often, he will attest to having 'huge muscular thighs' or 'buns of steel'. 'I like sex and sex likes me' is another phrase he will use.

6. *He is ignorant of basic protocols.* This is perhaps most evident in the question: 'Would anybody like to see my doodle?' This question is not accepted in most circles.

7. *He is living in a past age and gets things horribly wrong.* Sometimes, in a 'discotheque', he will request a song by Swedish group 'Bass of Ace'.

8. *He speaks 'Eurenglish' (or Not-Quite English).* 'I like to make party' is one of his lines, as is 'Would you very much like to make a photo of me?' And everything is Euro. 'Excuse me,' he will ask, 'do you love…(insert Eurovision, Europop, Eurostar or even EuroDisney—whichever is most irrelevant to the current topic)?'

So, as you can see, Oopsi really is a total wanker. But he is such fun to play, especially in a city where nobody knows you. That night he spoke to groups on the steps of Sacré Coeur, he haggled with nightclub owners, he sang to bars and he did stand-up comedy. We had an enormous Saturday night, most of which was in the area of the Moulin Rouge. I can remember few details, though I do remember Vic and I sitting at an outdoor café at eight in the morning with our shirts off (she had a bra on) waiting for breakfast to be served. After I freakishly met a guy on the street that I had played tennis with in Canberra when I was a teenager, we returned to the hotel, just in time to grab our gear. There would be no sleep for us until we got to Longchamps racetrack. Here we fell asleep under a tree for two hours, thereby totally missing out on the supposed purpose of our weekend away.

I have found that when a large group of people, who know each other to varying and sometimes limited degrees, go away for a period of time, one or more of them, almost invariably, do not fit in. I have also found that when this does happen, it can add a little bit of extra spice to the proceedings. In this respect, our Paris tour did not disappoint.

Stephen Norris was a figure regarded with some suspicion— verging on contempt—at Slothwick Skool. I tried to like him, even giving him a nickname—Chuck—that remains in common usage to this day. Chuck Norris adopted an overly confrontational stance in many of his dealings with students. He would frequently have 'brain snaps' and would swear at them or pick fights with them by 'chesting up'. As tempting as this behaviour was for all of us at times, the question needed to be asked of Chuck: 'Are you sure you're in the right job, mate?' The powers-that-be were aware of his tendency to totally lose it and had counselled him on the errors of his ways. He had managed to keep his temper under control—only just—but it was never far from the surface.

Quite apart from his poor relationship with many of the students, Chuck had managed to get on the wrong side of just about every member of staff in his short time at the school. He earned himself a reputation for being all 'huff and puff', and for doing very little of any worth or substance. His actions were highly unpredictable. Once, quite early on in my stay, I naively accepted his offer of a lift home from work. Turkish and another guy did the same, and the three of us sat holding on for dear life as he careered down the motorway in this little red VW Golf at about one hundred and thirty kilometres per hour. I swear, this thirty year old shitbox was on the verge of spontaneous combustion. As we got into the pedestrian zone of Hitchin, Chuck was forced to pull the reins on the thing. A group of seventeen year old students were crossing the road in front and, as we were about to find out, they were doing this a little too slowly for Chuck's liking.

'Hurry the fuck up or I'll kick you in the fucking head!' he roared out the window. Fortunately, we weren't required to dig him out of a hole, but it was a watershed moment for me. I would avoid him as much as I possibly could from this point. In one afternoon, he had demonstrated two disturbing behaviours. At thirty-seven, he was showing off in his car like a seventeen year old, and he was starting things he couldn't finish because he believed we would be there to bail him out. Pathetic.

Some months after this incident, his hot-headed nature landed him in much deeper trouble. When he was allegedly cut off by a female motorist in the car park of a Stevenage supermarket, he responded in true Chuck style, getting out of his car and letting her have it with several mouthfuls of obscenities. She had the presence of mind to read his nametag, which he had of course neglected to remove after his day at work, and note that he worked at the school that her daughter attended. One phone call to the head teacher later, and Chuck was undergoing compulsory anger management sessions.

In Paris, Chuck was true to form. He sought controversy from the outset, hoping to create a 'them and us' mentality—fourteen of us versus him and a crazy female South African teacher who was also very difficult to warm to. We were surprised that the pair of them elected to come on the trip, but we were truly prepared to give them a go. Unfortunately, they found it impossible to act in a way that even approached accepted social behaviour. On the first night, Chuck disappeared, only to return an hour later claiming he'd been mugged while trying to buy some 'snow'.[8] Next, it was his friend's turn to disappear—the mix of karaoke, laughter and alcohol obviously not doing it for her. She went off with two bikies, rejoining the group in the morning.

Chuck claimed that he spent four hours in a police cell on the Saturday night. It was funny, because normally one would be overcome with curiosity and pity if something like this happened to somebody they knew. With Chuck, we just said, 'Really?' and went on enjoying ourselves. He outdid himself on the return Eurostar journey, allegedly reporting us to the train staff for being too loud. This led to a scene in which train staff remonstrated with us. Chuck's role in this came out after our return, and I don't know whether to believe it or not. At London's King's Cross station on the way home, Chuck became detached from the group and informed us later that he had been, yet again, beaten up. This one I'm inclined to believe, because twice in the following week the police visited the school to interview him. I understand that they had accused him of trying to buy drugs. The supreme irony in all this is that Chuck, a man who could barely go a day without controversy, aggression or violence, has another life as a supposed DJ. He calls himself 'Natural Buddha', and when one checks out his website (as we did out of curiosity) one reads the phrase 'Peace and

[8] Cocaine. Once he said to me: 'So, Mr Fowler, is it going to be snowing for you this Christmas?'

deep beats' scrolling across the bottom of the screen. Perhaps it should read 'Police and deep beatings'.

Now that I'm on a roll, I think I will dedicate the rest of this chapter to assassinating a few more characters; none of whom took part in the Paris tour. Subtitle: *Clowns I Have Met.*

Chuck was a good buddy of another misfit at the school. 'Big Doug' was a huge (though not as huge as his son, who I'm certain was a Grizzly) Canadian bloke in his late fifties. Without his wife for the first few months of his stay in the UK, we could never really work out why he was bothering to go through the hell he was at Slothwick (and, believe me, he really did it tough). He was a geography teacher and so liked to travel. Perhaps he also needed the money. Vaughan likes to tell the story of Doug's first day in the country.

On that day, Doug rang Vaughan, introduced himself and asked when the two of them could meet. Vaughan invited him round that evening for dinner with him and his wife, also inviting the school's other geography teacher and her husband.

'7.00 p.m. okay?" asked Vaughan.

'Let's make it earlier,' suggested Doug.

'Well, I can't really. We've got quite a bit on in the afternoon. Seven is best for us.'

Doug turned up at 1.30 p.m., in a car that he'd bought that morning, before proceeding to get pissed and bore the living shit out of everybody by telling them how big and great everything is in Canada. Come midnight, after a day of drinking, 'the big man' announced his intention to drive back to his lodgings. This left Vaughan with a moral dilemma. Doug would almost certainly crash and kill somebody on the way home, but was this worth it not to have him at the house for breakfast? In the end, Vaughan did the responsible thing.

Doug's laissez-faire approach to the mixing of driving and alcohol consumption reared its head time and time again throughout the year, and (despite the efforts of many to talk him out of this behaviour) I don't think he ever caught a taxi. He was even pissed at the school's open night; red-faced and buddying up to total strangers. We all took turns at going to his classroom to watch him. He was often a source of great amusement, especially when he was asked where he was living. We had friends of ours ask him, just to watch the response. It was always identical:

'Doug, where do you live?'

(In a strong Canadian accent) 'Kimpton.'

'Where is that?'

(Pointing to an imaginary map in front of his face, like a true geography teacher) 'London's here…Luton's here…Stevenage is here…Knebworth's here…and Kimpton's here.'

It was extremely difficult to keep a straight face when you were hearing it for the twenty-seventh time. He was just so serious about it.

Joining Chuck and Doug as the third stooge was a little dweeby fellow called Clive Head. I was far more inclined to feel sorry for 'Clive Headjob' (as we usually called him) than I was for the other two. His behaviour was certainly strange but, unlike the other two, he was completely harmless—unless you count the fact that he was providing very few meaningful learning experiences to students due to his inability to control the class. I believe the most power-ful weapon a teacher has in his or her arsenal is their personality, and Clive Head just didn't have one. But what he did have was a girlfriend, and he made sure that everybody knew it. As a thirty-six year old semi-qualified teacher (who actually failed to qualify just prior to me leaving)[9], Clive Head was dating one of the school's cleaners—a nineteen year old. And it was obvious to all that she wasn't entirely faithful. She was often seen flirting horrendously

[9] Teachers are in such short supply in Britain that they are using people who are not yet fully qualified.

with a Year 10 student—in fact, I saw them kiss in the car park one afternoon. It gets worse. Clive Head ate 'Breakfast in a Can' and (get this) he ate it at lunchtime. For the uneducated, this is a delectable fusion of scrambled eggs, bacon and sausage, poured from a can into a hot pan, and then, to the colon's delight, eaten. Clive Head ate it often in the staffroom, when he wasn't eating toast. Boy, could he put the toast away, and always with bloody marmalade. It didn't shut him up though. He was expert at interjecting and thereby killing a conversation. The general pattern was: joke, laughter, joke, laughter, Clive Head boring trivial fact, silence. He was the sort of bloke who thought he knew everything, though, as his life betrayed, he patently did not. His conversations were everybody's conversations, because he had absolutely no control over the volume of his voice. Once, he bellowed at somebody for five minutes about ironing. I think we were all too depressed to put a stop to it. One day he told me that, as he walked to school, he had seen some graffiti concerning me on a fence. I was interested in seeing the alleged penning of 'Fowler is gay', thinking that it might make a good photo, so I asked him to show it to me. Turns out that it read: 'Bowyer [a well-known footballer] is gay'. Now either Clive Head can't read, or he just wanted to go for a walk with me. He really was a silly chap, but he didn't deserve the eggings his house (which was literally adjacent to the school) received periodically from Slothwick students.

A member of staff who took poor Clive Head under her wing was an Australian, whom we knew not so affectionately as 'Mad Sal'. Sal, as Clive Head's self-appointed relationship counsellor, helped the poor bloke over many a rocky bump. And, when things were on the skids, she'd try to set him up with someone she'd met on a train or in a supermarket. This service seemed (initially at least) to be completely free of charge.

Sal had crawled out from a rock somewhere in Queensland, and found herself a job at Slothwick soon after I did. Something I've learned over the years is that when you're new to a place, you sit tight for a while, keep your nose out of things and try to get a general feel for the lie of the land. Mad Sal had not learnt that lesson. The first time any of us saw her was when she blew into the staffroom like a tornado and started to loudly butt into people's professional conversations. She confirmed all of the Brits' stereotypes about Australians—loud, uncouth, slovenly—and it was embarrassing for me to be around her. Within days, she had converted the 'prep room' (an annex off the staffroom with two computers, where people were supposed to be able to work quietly) into an Internet café. She attracted a couple of like-minded ladies into her clique, and there they would sit—whingeing, bitching and gossiping till the cows came home. I don't think any of them did any work at all.

Every morning and afternoon, I would be forced to enter their lair in order to access my locker. Sal would always try to start up a conversation with me, regardless of how busy or flustered I looked. She was one of those people who asked questions (and usually inane ones) and then provided her own answers. She really didn't seem interested in my answers at all, which always made me wonder why she had bothered to ask the questions in the first place. Our conversations would generally run something like this:

Her: 'G'day Glenno.'

Me: 'Hi Sal.'

Her: 'Whadya get up to on the weekend? Go to London? Yeah. Did ya go out? I'll bet you did, hey. Have a few drinks? Good one mate. Meet anyone? Any nice girls? Come on, a nice lookin' fella like you would be sure to meet a few nice girls. What's happening this weekend? Going away? Nuh, saving your money for the hols huh? Good on ya mate. Sounds like a good plan. I went with Mum to Oxford. Christ, she was carrying on the whole bloody way. It was a good day but probably not as exciting as yours, I bet. Whadya reckon?'

Me: 'Probably not, Sal.'

When I was permitted to answer, I generally gave one-syllable ones. I knew for a fact that she gossiped about me, like she did about everybody else. I wasn't going to give her any more ammunition than she already had.

One of her cronies was another Aussie named Patty. Patty was actually all right, if a bit highly strung. Her worst side came out when she was around Sal. They would convince each other that the world was against them, they would constantly complain about Britain, and they were obsessed with trying to rationalise the fact that neither of them could get a man. This last fact was hardly surprising, as both were old before their time, and their dress sense conveyed that—olive slacks with navy blazers on most days.

I know a lot about what was said in the prep room from Vic, who, towards the end, began to do the odd reconnaissance mission. Their advice to her was to: 'Get yourself a man like Dil, Vic…a man like Dil!' (Dilbert was the fiancé of a girl on staff that we all liked.) Vic would politely agree, before listening in as they badmouthed every male on the staff. According to Patty, all male teachers treat women badly because they are making up for the fact that they are in a feminine profession and this hurts their sense of masculinity. Sal's philosophy was a little simpler: 'Men are shits!' (or 'sheets' as she pronounced it).

In the last few weeks, we started to have a bit of fun with Sal. Vic and I decided to give some credence to her theories on men. Vic created a scenario in which I was trying to have my way with her (Vic, not Sal!), and was becoming more and more brazen about it. When she told her that I had deliberately brushed up against her with an erection, Sal responded with, 'Geez Vic! He's a horny bugger!' The twist was provided when Vic started to admit to *liking* this fictional behaviour of mine. I don't think Sal knew what was going on at the time. But she continued to tell her cronies about me, and soon I had quite a reputation. At least she left me alone.

Turkish and Mike came to the party by having some MENAR Sheets ('Men are sheets') printed off and selectively distributed. (MENAR was an acronym for the nonsensical Management in Education New Action Report.) When completed, teachers were to place these in the MENAR Sheets box above computer number two, at which Sal sat every day coordinating what seemed to be more or less a dating agency.

The kids at Slothwick thought Sal was as 'balmy' as we did. This could have been helped by the fact that she would often pad out her RE lessons with renditions of 'He's Got The Whole World In His Hands' or 'Rock My Soul In The Bosom Of Abraham', complete with dancing and theatrics. The general consensus on Patty was a little more positive. One kid said: 'Miss Montrose is so attractive—she could be a porn star!' Now there's a wrap.

Barry John worked with my flatmate Grace at Buzzardsbeak and attended one or two of our social events. He seemed a fairly innocuous sort of bloke, and the fact that he was from Melbourne meant that we could at least talk about the footy. The two of us got chatting one day and he mentioned that he had nothing planned for an upcoming long weekend. I told him that I intended to hire a car and check out England's West Country, and that he should think about coming along for the ride. I was able to convince Grace to join us, and another female friend made four.

On the first night, we found ourselves in Torquay—the setting for *Fawlty Towers*. It was difficult to find accommodation on that Saturday night, on account of the fact that Torquay seemed to be the buck's (stag's) and hen's night capital of the universe. (We saw a whole busload of girls dressed up as policewomen…sexy.) We eventually found a place and Barry and I ended up having to share a double bed. This didn't really bother me, but I was conscious enough of the need for my own personal space to carefully construct a 'pillow wall' between us. I didn't think this was so weird, but my friends seemed to think it was a scream. A couple of months later, many were hailing me as a visionary for having accurately pegged a bloke of highly questionable tendencies.[10]

On the first of the big nights out in Hitchin to which Barry was a party, he disappeared, only to be found hours later, asleep on my doorstep. This time, the benefit of the doubt was duly granted. On another such occasion, Vic and Patty (who was significantly more bearable minus Mad Sal) ended up sleeping on sofa beds in our lounge room. In the wee small hours, the pair was suddenly woken by the noise of somebody moving feverishly nearby. As it turned out, it was Barry—and he was 'sleep-wanking'. Patty screamed, Vic kicked him in the stomach, and he fell between them. Patty raced upstairs looking for me. She got as far as Grace's room, where Grace was conscripted to descend the stairs to pull him…into line. (I couldn't resist—sorry.) You'd think the next morning he would have been mortified to know that he had done such a thing. On the contrary, his response was that the girls 'should have been flattered', and instead of leaving with his tail between his legs, he hung around (my God, I'm trying hard to resist further puns here) and joined us at breakfast. And he put up with the million and one jokes about sausages and cream! ('Hand me the sausages, Barry.')

One thing I liked was that Vaughan refused—for some time—to believe that the guy's name is Barry John. Barry John is apparently the name of a Welsh rugby legend so, as Vaughan believed, it could not be possible for anybody else to have the same name. We told Vaughan that he had been named after the rugby player and that his Christian name was actually 'Barryjohn'—Barryjohn Smyth being his full name. This led Vaughan to call him Barryjohn to his face, creating all sorts of carefully disguised mirth. It only goes to prove

---

[10] Our trip to the West Country is mentioned again in Chapter Ten, with a slightly more cultural focus.

that even very intelligent people like Vaughan can be taken for a ride—in the name of humour.

Given that this chapter has turned out to be chiefly about strange and/or unlikeable people, I cannot complete it without mentioning my contact at the recruitment agency with which I was employed. This bastard schmoozed me on the phone before I left Australia, and promptly forgot about me as soon as I arrived. He returned almost none of my calls and almost none of my emails. The exceptions were when he stood to gain from doing so. He stuffed up my pay on more than one occasion, causing me great inconvenience, and was unable to rectify the fault. He made every excuse under the sun, and then used a few from beyond the sun. I know for a fact that he treated others with the same contempt, and these people were more than happy to provide evidence for an official complaint that I made. I understand that he earned double my income—not surprising when you consider that his agency was taking a *third* of my daily wage. Yet, at a get-together arranged for the recruits of the agency in London one Friday night, the rank and file (us) did not get a brass razoo. At one point, this fat prick stood next to me at the bar, said hello, bought two beers, skulled one, sipped from the next and walked away. To anybody planning to teach through an agency in Britain, my advice to you is simple: do your research and be wary. And to my agent (whom I will refrain from naming), I have this to say. It is my dream to one day make more money writing books about scumbags like you than you make from ripping off people like me. Oh, and one more thing...fuck you!

Eight
Scandinavia: Journeying to the Top of Europe...Then Trying to Work Out Why

Flushed with the success of my first Contiki tour, I thought I'd go back for more in July/August. I'd always wanted to see Scandinavia, because it was *there* more than anything, and a tour like this seemed the only way I'd be able to afford it. You may have heard stories about how expensive the place is and, now that I've been there, I can confirm that these stories are true. In Norway, in an average small town pub, you will pay between ten and twelve Australian dollars for a pint of beer (or at least it would be a pint if they filled it to the top). Alcohol, in particular, is taxed heavily for two reasons. First, it dissuades people from drinking it and thereby spiralling into a life of uselessness and, secondly and most importantly, the tax revenue is used to help fund the 'cradle to the grave' welfare system—a system that sees parents and pensioners cared for to a degree that is both astounding and enviable. One example is maternity leave provisions, which allow mothers *and* fathers to take advantage of extended periods of paid leave. It's tough for tourists though, who pay the exorbitant prices without reaping the benefits. Essentials like food seem to be better priced, but luxury items don't bear thinking about. The price of this three-week trip seemed very reasonable (around 1000 pounds or A$2500), until I found out what we were getting for our money.

I made two very close Australian friends on this trip with whom I continue to catch up. Col and House, both originally from

Melbourne and mates for about ten years, are mentioned in the following pages, but publicising some of what the three of us got up to would probably send us straight to hell. Three weeks on a bus, travelling up to fourteen hours a day, accompanied by some of the most insecure, naive and desperate individuals on the planet, and being forced every morning to listen to a 'tour song' that would drive Mother Theresa to homicide, can do strange things to three well-meaning blokes. House put his finger on it towards the end of the trip:

'I've worked out why we've become animals. They treat us like animals. You can't go driving people around all day, putting them in stables or concentration camps every night and feeding them Pal [a brand of dog food]. Look what we've become. Look at our hair, our filthy habits. And just listen to us…'

In fact, on the night of debauchery otherwise known as the Viking Party, where we were encouraged to eat our meat and vegies with our fingers, I don't think we even noticed we were doing it.

On the marathon bus journeys, card games and trivia quizzes soon lost their appeal, and we were reduced to seeing who could write the most depraved poem or who could offend the most people by altering song lyrics. (House won, but only because the Beatles' 'Baby You Can Drive My Car' was made for this game.) Most of our conversations were infantile at best, and nobody could quite work out why (when we weren't sleeping or crying) we were laughing so often. It was too hard to explain to them then and it would be too hard to explain to you now. One example of our lack of maturity was the night at Mo I Rana in Norway when House suggested we go on a 'panty raid' (like this was something that one routinely did) and, despite being thirty years of age, I didn't require much convincing. Fuelled by beer[11], we performed

---

[11] We had been playing '100 Club', where you have to drink a shot (30ml) of beer every minute for one hundred minutes without getting up to go to the toilet.

the deed, before excitedly returning to what we thought was our cabin, knocking feverishly on the glass door and screaming at the other blokes to let us in. This turned out to be a miscalculation. Foiled by the identical nature of the cabins, we were actually banging on the door of the tour leader, who was actually rather unimpressed. We ran to the correct cabin and, like naughty boys on a school camp, peered from behind the curtains as she (playfully I think) shook her finger at us from our porch. The following day, precious little was said about the raid by her or the victims, who had simply collected their items of underwear from the central set of kiddy swings where we had left them and got on with their day. We expected a stinging act of revenge, but it never really came. Later that morning, the tour leader walked down the bus with three items of underwear that had not been claimed. I thought House was joking when he kept shouting: 'Those black ones are Col's!' Turns out he wasn't. One of the guys, Ron, had gone way overboard, collecting every garment he could find south of the Arctic Circle and Col, who was asleep at the time, was caught in the crossfire—or at least his undies were. The next night, I became the subject of laughter when my trousers caught alight as I stood over the embers of the camp fire roasting nuts.

Everything in Scandinavia is perfectly ordered, impeccably clean, peace-promoting and environmentally friendly (except for the whaling in Norway), in a way that is reminiscent of Japan. These nations have got their shit together. They really know how to look after their own backyard and, because of economic prosperity and the resultant high living standards, are invariably rated amongst the top few countries in which to live. Culturally, though, I found the place not deprived, but somewhat lacking. Scandinavians, from my observations, are much like Scandinavia —impressive but bland.

The Italians, the Spanish and other southern European or Mediterranean peoples are very up-front with their emotions.

They wear their hearts on their sleeves and exude colour, passion and spontaneity. Things occur randomly and without warning. People in restaurants start singing or dancing for no apparent reason. Women argue with their husbands in front of strangers, occasionally turning to these strangers for some endorsement. Couples flock to parks on perfect sunny days to publicly kiss, caress and God knows what else. These people will not die wondering. For all of their faults—their inefficiencies, their unhelpfulness and their inability to be diplomatic—these southern Europeans are a pleasure to be amongst. They put a show on for you every day, and their zest for life starts to course through your veins as well.

The Scandinavians are a very different breed. Centuries of staying indoors during winters of no warmth and very little sunlight; frugally hoarding supplies and fraternising with very few has made them a more sedate and insular bunch. They are not unadventurous—just look at the Vikings who discovered North America five hundred years before Columbus...oh...and Ikea—tell me those guys aren't furniture trailblazers. It's just that the Scandinavians are so practical...so sensible. I've already mentioned the nature of their welfare systems. They seem to be obsessed with the idea of saving for a rainy day (or, more accurately, three months of dark, bitterly cold days). If the gloves truly came off and the countries of the world found themselves locked in a battle for survival, I reckon you'd be wise to put a few dollars on a Scandinavian country. They'd be there at the finish, busily storing and planning. (The Italians and Spanish—the latter long propped up by the EU—would probably be among the first to fold.) The Scandinavians are clever, polite and healthy people who are impressive to behold. Somehow, though, they're just not *silly* enough. Fortunately, the visit of our tour group compensated for this deficiency.

The first part of our Scandinavia trip consisted of a series of city tours, as all of the capital cities are in the southern areas. Crossing an amazing twenty-kilometre bridge into the pretty and very walkable Copenhagen, I found the Danish capital to be typically northern European. I was quite taken by a large statue of four crocodiles with tails intertwined, symbolising the closeness of the four Scandinavian countries.

Part of my impetus to get to Scandinavia was the desire to see Stockholm, about which I had heard so many glowing reports. Stockholm sits among dozens of islands and, along with Paris, Sydney, New York and (if photographs don't lie) Rio de Janeiro, truly is one of the most spectacular cities on Earth. Gamla Stan, or the Old Town, provides excellent meandering possibilities, a chance to see the changing of the Royal Guard, and views of surrounding peninsulas adorned with gorgeous residences and public buildings. Cruise boat tours provide a different perspective on this scenic wonder, along with the opportunity to constantly adjust other people's headset controls so that they hear the commentary in Swedish, Italian, Spanish, French or German. The transition between languages is perfectly seamless and it is fun to see how many seconds it takes for the victim to realise.

Stockholm, like all Scandinavian and many northern European cities, provides some excellent opportunities for 'mullet-hunting'. Be it long and curly, long and straight, with or without accompanying spike or shaved sides, these people really know how to grow a mullet. In the time I was there, I saw two 'Squirrel Pelts' and even a rare 'Kentucky Waterfall'! A top vantage point for spotting mullets, and even for having a look over Stockholm, is the Town Hall. This is where the Nobel prizes are awarded each year, and it was good to get a feel for the podium—just in case. I'd like to say that I learned a lot about Stockholm from our female guide at the Town Hall, but I'd be lying. All I learned is that the rumours of Swedish girls being complete babes are true. All twelve guys on the tour, and probably some of the thirty-six girls, spent the entire tour gazing helplessly at this woman and trying to prevent tongues from reaching the floor. We didn't listen to a word she said. Dan, true to form, videotaped her—and only her—for no less than twenty minutes.

The Town Hall's tower provides an incredible three hundred and sixty-degree view of the city, and on the descent, I discovered a piece of inspiration from a graffiti 'artist'. On one of the bricks was scribbled the word 'sex'. Not 'I like sex' or 'Sex is great'—just 'sex'. This is right up there with some of my favourites—'penis' on a Sydney footpath and 'fuck' on a Canberra road sign. Exactly what are these people thinking? The only possible explanations are that the perpetrators are six years old, or members of a secret Make Glenn Laugh Society (MGLS).

I've always had a comical interest in graffiti (though none in actually producing it), since one particular example had an impact on me as a young child. For years, an underpass near my parents' house in Canberra was home to the words 'Drink more piss!' The first time I saw this was one of those real 'end of innocence' moments. I thought to myself: 'What on Earth would possess somebody to write that? There must be some sick people around.' Perhaps not surprisingly, given my age, I thought the author of this work was suggesting we should drink more urine. The penny dropped perhaps around the age of twelve when I realised that we were being told to drink more alcohol ('piss' being a colloquial term for such). I found this new understanding less disturbing and more amusing. Here was someone who had discovered the secret to a happy life and was prepared to share it with all and sundry. Strangely enough, as you might have guessed, I've recently followed these words of wisdom, on some occasions to the nth degree.

On this tour I was finding it increasingly difficult to 'drink more piss', and I felt it was one of the only things that was going to help me survive this largely inane, party-pooping bunch. The price of liquor, as you know, was a problem, but it was matched by the fiendish location of the majority of our camp sites. After finding ourselves at basic (and obviously cheap) lodgings an hour out of the cities of Copenhagen and Stockholm, we found the same thing at the Norwegian capital, Oslo. The boys and I agreed that we would rather have paid more for the tour in order to stay somewhere relatively central. We made the effort to travel into town on some nights, but on others we were simply too shagged from the bus travel and late arrival.

Oslo is an elegant city with a few things worth seeing. Gustav Vigeland's sculptures in Frognerparken are stunning, adding to one's appreciation of the human form. Statues abound of men, women, children, families, lovers and friends; and Col and House became intimate with many of these for the sake of an amusing snapshot. The centrepiece of the park is an enormous column consisting of dozens of writhing bodies, apparently the world's largest granite sculpture. The menacing boats at Oslo's Viking Museum are worth checking out, as are Thor Heyerdahl's rafts at the Kon-Tiki Museum. On several occasions, between the late 1940s and early 1970s, Heyerdahl and his teams set off in these rafts to show that the indigenous peoples of the Americas may not have been as isolated as first thought, and may have had meaningful contact with Europeans and also Pacific Islanders. Somerset Maugham described one of Heyerdahl's expeditions as 'an incredible adventure which happens to be true'.

To Contiki's credit, we did and saw some cool things during the first few days in Norway. One experience that I won't be telling my osteopath about was our bobsled ride at Lillehammer, host city for the 1994 Winter Olympics. This was totally ridiculous. I was at the back of the four-person contraption as we flew down the course at one hundred and sixty kilometres per hour. The ride lasted just over a minute, but after fifteen seconds all I remember is trying to stop the front of my helmet from hitting Col's (this was all I could see) and trying to stop the back of it from hitting the surrounding cage. My efforts were to no avail. I became a slave to the machine and just hung on for dear life, waiting for it to be over. At one point I felt my entire spine contract, and it took me about ten minutes to get over the strain of it. One very fit woman had trouble walking for three days!

The nearby ski jump was interesting, as was the fact that people were using it without snow. I had no idea that they trained on artificial grass during the summer months. The act of performing the ski jump looked like an incredible buzz, though I would never have the intestinal fortitude to attempt it.

These insights into Nordic sports gave me cause to further refine my theories on the Scandinavian people. I think it is fitting that the stoic Scandinavians are the best in the world at sports in which the participant doesn't move. In ski jumping, you stand (or lean) as still and as stony-faced as you can. In the luge and the bobsled, you just lie or sit there, you shut up (and you certainly don't argue with any referees) and you wait until the terror is over. Look at the way the Scandinavians play football (soccer). They are very good at it, but their best attributes are mental and physical strength, fitness, clinical precision and the ability to not stuff up. They defend, they defend and they defend a bit more. They're...so sensible. Meanwhile, the southern Europeans are running around belting people, taking dives all over the place, and berating and assaulting the referee. But when they're not rolling around in agony, crying with joy or pashing a team-mate, they are exhibiting outrageous flair and scoring brilliantly flamboyant goals. They are taking risks and pushing the envelope. But, unlike the Scandinavians, they stuff things up and they let in goals by not being careful enough. Of course, Africans and South Americans play in a similar fashion (the Spanish and Portuguese elements undoubtedly influencing the latter), and again I put it down to the mindsets and lifestyles of the people. I think it is fascinating that climate not only has a profound influence on the way people are (more on this when

I discuss the Poms in Chapter Eleven), but also on the sports that they are good at and even the way they play them. And, I contend, on the cars they make. The Italians produce the Ferrari. It is stylish, loud, brash, and cries out: 'Look at me.' The Swedes produce the Volvo. It is safe, reliable and practical. It is...so sensible. It will see you through the winter, but you won't be picking up any chicks. Still, if nobody is outside to look at your car, who cares how boring it looks?

Svartisen Glacier, Norway's second largest, was worth the boat ride and long rock walk. I'd never seen a glacier before, and was awestruck by it. The highlight was when part of the end of it fell off, producing an almighty racket and some serious ripples in the adjacent lake. It was one of those moments when the power of nature was overwhelming.

It was at this point that our group commenced a five-day haul in the bus. The objective was to make it to Hammerfest, the northernmost city in Europe, and a base for the trek to Nordkapp ('North Cape')—the northernmost point of Europe. Hammerfest itself was a place bereft of any charm, and the site for our camp site was clearly chosen by somebody who intended to live nearby, sit on his verandah and, with the aid of binoculars, laugh hysterically at unhappy inmates as they slipped down rocky outcrops and had their heads blown off by Arctic gales. For us, Hammerfest became 'Bumfuck, Idaho' (a 'Twelfth Man' reference) or occasionally 'Jerkwater, USA' (from Stallone's *First Blood*).

The 'optional' (What else would we do?!) post-dinner trip to Nordkapp was a nightmare. I don't know what was worse—three hours in the bus in total darkness (after ten hours on the road that day), a view toward the Arctic consisting wholly of thick fog, or the insistence of some on the tour to pose for the cameras with their genitals hanging out. Actually, probably the worst thing was getting only four hours sleep after all of the above.

I had been persuaded, against my better judgement, to put aside my passionate disinterest in fishing and fear of seasickness and sign up for the next day's 'deep sea fishing' excursion. Thankfully, as it turned out, we didn't even leave the bay. On pulling anchor, hand lines were handed out to about half of the participants, who proceeded to catch fish at an incredible rate. To me, as an observer, it didn't look like much of a challenge. After five minutes of sheer boredom, I thought I might go below deck and take a seat for a few minutes. The events of the previous night had obviously taken it out of me. I was woken two hours later by the sound of the boat docking, realising that one hundred Australian dollars was the most I had ever paid for a short kip.

Having reached the end of the earth, we needed to make our way down to Helsinki, the capital of Finland. It was on the second of two full days driving through the Finnish countryside, which consiste wholly and solely of pine trees, that I started to contemplate whether the tour designers had got it right. I never thought I'd see a country with *too many* trees, but now I have. At times, I would have killed to see a bitumen car park. In truth, those two days of bus travel to and three days from Nordkapp yielded very little return. We saw a bit more scenery (though no more spectacular than we had seen previously), a few more reindeers and many more petrol stations. I contend that that part of the tour is unnecessary. Nordkapp is simply not worth the effort, especially when it is too foggy to see a damned thing.

By the time we emerged from what has to be the world's largest forest, House, Col and I were starting to get the shits. With the exceptions of Ron (who had, by now, formed a tight relationship with a girl on the bus), Dan (who was murdering more brain cells by the day, due to his penchant for attaching himself to mad vodka-drinking Ukrainians in caravan parks), and a couple of girls who were good value, the tour group was adding to our frustrations. The members of the self-appointed ruling triumvirate—or the Axis of Evil, as we called them—were beginning to bare their fangs. House and I had consistently spurned the advances of one, while another was still smarting from Col's rejection of her way back in Denmark. The third didn't really know what to think, but was soon told exactly what to think. The influence that they wielded among the other females on the bus was considerable, and our names were becoming closer and closer to mud. By the time we reached Finland, where we would separate (more than half of the group continuing on to Russia while the rest of us headed back to England), these ladies were starting to play hard-ball, hiding our football (sacrilege I know), and getting to the bus early in the morning to occupy our seats and gloat over it. They thought they hated us. As we were about to find out, though, they actually loved to hate us (or hated to love us, I'm not sure).

As we approached civilisation, in the form of a town called Rovaniemi, the three of us were discussing the possibility of leaving the group and spending a couple of days in Sweden. House runs a backpackers' hostel in Sydney, and in his time has met plenty of Swedes. A couple of them lived in a town called Kalix just over the border, and they happened to be hot little blondes, not all that uncommon for Swedish women. Eventually, we decided that leaving the group would be too difficult, both time-wise and money-wise, but we organised to meet the Swedes, along with a couple of their friends, at our camp site *just outside* Rovaniemi. (As if we'd actually stay *in* somewhere.) From there, we would go out and see what this town had to offer.

Well, you should have seen the reaction of the captain, vice-captain and mascot of Bitches United when the bus rolled in to the camp site and four beautiful blondes in a BMW were waiting for us. These three oxygen thieves, all pride sacrificed, proceeded to hang around us like bad smells as we hurriedly preened ourselves, taking immense satisfaction from the fact that the showers were occupied by a group of Latvian carnies, restricting us to a rather unpleasant cold wash. They reminded us that we would be passing up a Christmas Party at the reputed home of Santa, and that we would therefore miss out on the random exchange of ten-dollar (Australian) gifts. (As it turned out, all we missed out on was World War III, as fights erupted between these childlike creatures over who was entitled to which gift). As devastated as I was by the cruel twist of fate that would cause me to miss this event, I consoled myself with the fact that I would be able to keep the t-shirt I purchased at a roadside market bearing a great big pair of boobs on the front. (Note to self: I must get more wear out of that shirt.)

The only bummer as we left the camp site was that there were seven of us (Me, Col, House and the four Swedish girls) needing to squeeze in to a five-seater car. You can't imagine how terrible it was for me to be pressed up against these people whom I had only just met. (Okay, I'll stop now.)

Rolling into nearby Rovaniemi, we fronted up to a club/restaurant that turned out to be an experience in itself. I guess it was something like the Finnish equivalent of a Returned Servicemen's Club. Totally devoid of any style, it was how I imagined frontier areas of the old Soviet Union to have been like. After some frivolous chatting, it was down to business—ballroom dancing! This was great fun, even though the musical accompaniment left a little to be desired. Imagine Elvis—but a really old Elvis, with a beard, and really uncool, and virtually unable to move...actually, just forget Elvis. Imagine a bunch of Rasputins with electric guitars. Now you've got it.

After being kicked out for being under sixty years of age, we discovered that there was a karaoke bar in the building. I felt it drawing me in, like many a karaoke bar has done before.

My first karaoke experience was as an eighteen year old at my football club in Canberra. It still amazes me that I volunteered to sing, particularly when I consider that I was stone cold sober.

(I didn't touch a drop of alcohol until I was twenty.) Maybe I didn't have a choice about singing—I'm a bit vague on this. Anyway, to a packed club I nervously started to sing Joan Jett's 'I Love Rock and Roll', before really getting into it and padding out the instrumental section with a few back-breaking pelvic thrusts. Perhaps it was then I realised that I am a hopeless extrovert.

The thing is: I actually *can* sing. I knew that when I was eighteen, which is why I must have agreed to walk on stage in a room full of older guys (and their partners) whose football ability and worldliness (or so I thought—it was probably just their age) made me feel insecure. I've sung semi-professionally in rock bands and duos ever since and have had the pleasure of singing at the weddings of several of my close friends. And I owe it all to karaoke!

It is my experience that, when it comes to clean, wholesome, unadulterated fun, karaoke nights rarely fail to deliver. (When I say wholesome, I neglect to mention the night I was asked by the manager of a Sydney karaoke restaurant to put my shirt back on and to stop whipping my own buttocks with my belt.) One night my friends and I went to the Woolloomooloo Bay Hotel, also in Sydney, to grab something to eat. Coming back through the nightclub after our feed, my friends started to pester me to knock out a tune. I was tired and a little under the weather, but I eventually agreed to do a song, with one condition—it had to be George Michael's 'Faith'. A few minutes later, I was performing the song, and the extrovert in me had taken over once more. This time, it was an air guitar solo. When the song finished, we were about to leave when they started to announce the finalists:

'Ladies and gentlemen, put your hands together for John...and Claudia...and Glenn!'

Now here's what's funny about karaoke. There is a sub-culture in our society, comprising people like John and Claudia, who take their karaoke extremely seriously. They travel from nightclub to nightclub, maintain a strict sobriety (like a normal person does at work) and try to bring home the bacon. This John bloke was on first name terms with the host. It was his beat. And you should have seen him. He'd done his best to look like U2's Bono, purchasing a black, ankle-length coat and standing out in the wind for a couple of hours to make himself look rugged. He was a *nose-scruncher* from way back (scrunch your nose up and close your eyes—then you'll know what I mean) and he didn't mind throwing in the ol' clenched fist. Claudia too was not averse to punching the air when she hit the high notes of Bonnie Tyler's 'Total Eclipse of the Heart'. Both of them could sing, just not very well. I won and we got free alcohol over the bar. Needless to say, we didn't leave in a hurry.

The extension of karaoke, for me, has been asking professional bands if I can get up and sing with them. I pride myself on my ability to convince them that I'm not a total hacker and I won't 'smash their shit'. When a bunch of us were in Santiago, Chile for my mate Dominic's wedding in November 2000, we had dinner one night in a bar/restaurant. The drinks were flowing, a band was playing and I asked them if I could sing a song. They obliged, I sang, and then they went for a short break. During the break, the singer approached me and asked me if I knew 'Black' by Pearl Jam. I told him I did and we performed it. As I was leaving the stage, he stopped me and asked me if I knew 'Born To Be Wild'. I told him I knew the tune but I didn't know all of the words. 'No problem!' he exclaimed, producing a music stand and words to just about every song ever written. As it turned out, I did seven songs in a row—an entire set in fact. The more I have thought about it, the more I believe I was entitled to a cut of their earnings.

On Dom's buck's night, also in Santiago, we went to a club owned by these two Casanovas who looked like they could star in the Chilean version of *The Bold and the Beautiful*. They were on stage performing to a packed house, and the ladies were going wild at their hauntingly beautiful acoustic ballads. The next thing we could work out was that they were playing the national anthems of various countries (mostly South American of course) and pockets of people were singing along. Then, one of the guys—the one who looked like Ridge Forrester (one of the spunks from the aforementioned soap)—turned to us (a group of ten or more) and asked what country we hailed from. 'Australia!' was, of course, the reply and as he didn't know how to play it, we belted out the anthem without accompaniment. What we didn't realise was that this was all part of a competition, and, as it turned out, our entry was deemed adequate to book us a spot in the final. Given that we thought it must be a singing competition, the boys pushed me up on to the stage where I was joined by a large, bald headed gentleman, who I was later told was the Peruvian heavy-weight boxing champion. The host, Ridge, spoke to me in words I did not understand and I responded with: 'Do you know any Elvis?' He nodded reassuringly, pressed a button behind me, and ushered me centre stage. The next thing I heard was the opening bar of Joe Cocker's 'You Can Leave Your Hat On' (Dada da da da dada da da da), and I suddenly realised what was expected of me. As you've probably worked out by now, I'm hardly a shrinking violet, so the idea of stripping in front of a couple of hundred peo-ple did not present a huge hurdle. Thinking that I had three and a half minutes to get my gear off, I took it pretty slowly. When they stopped the song, after about a minute, I was standing there with my shirt off and my belt in my hand. (No, I hadn't started whipping my buttocks—I'm not a regular flagellant.) Next, it was the Peruvian's turn and, although he could have snapped me in two, he had the dancing ability of Pope John Paul II. Ridge was soon back on the mike. 'Peruvian?!' he asked the audience, 'or Australian?!!!' I got more cheers than the boxer and, once again, free booze was the reward.

At Dom's buck's night in Australia, held at the coastal town of Mollymook, I took to the stage at a pub called The Marlin with a bunch of hard rockers. After my song, the buck's party waited for me outside while I went to the toilet. As I emerged from the pub, I could see the boys milling around at the bottom of the stairs. I was following a girl down the stairs and as she reached the bottom, she asked them if they were the band. This question clearly came from somebody who had had a couple too many shandies—for a start, there were ten of them, plus they didn't look anything like the band...and the band were actually still playing inside.

'We sure are,' came the reply, 'and (pointing to me) that's the singer!' She turned around, told me I was awesome, kissed me on the lips and asked me to sign the band's CD, which she had obviously just purchased.

'To whom should I address it,' I asked, though probably not with such grammatical perfection.

'To me, Tammy,' she replied.

Looking carefully at the CD's credits, and noticing that the singer's name was Michael, I scrawled with a flurry: 'To Tim Tam, You love me, Michael.' The thought of her sobering up the next day and reading that crap slays me every time.

So, you ask, after all this, where is there for an extrovert to go? What mountains are left to climb? The answer: catwalk modelling.

In recent years, I've spent a fair bit of time with a guy called Rich, who shares my love for showing off. At twenty-five years of age, he is probably the most confident person I have ever met. You could throw him into any social situation with any calibre of person and he would be totally at ease. He specialises in celebrities, going straight for the jugular and asking the tough questions—be it AFL coach Kevin Sheedy, musician John Butler or even the brilliant Blair from *Big Brother* and *Neighbours*. One night we were out and, pretty much simultaneously, the two of us came up with the idea of modelling. Here's what you do. Enlist the help of a like-minded fruitcake (it works best with two), go into a nightclub, and then take it in turns to strut out on to centre stage. When you get there, hold (waiting…waiting…) and then strut back. Then your mate comes out and does the same. We started with very minimalist moves—just planting the feet, staring at the audience and then skipping away. We then introduced body-building poses, then stretching regimens and finally aerobics routines. Recently, we've reverted to minimalism, staring at the audience with contempt and even muttering arrogantly under our breath, as if to say: 'You philistines don't appreciate our work.' The punters generally take a while to work out what the hell is going on, before getting into it. And the bouncers don't seem to mind. Some of them even laugh, which, in my experience, is a rarity. For me, true comedy is when your subject doesn't know whether you're serious or not—that's what's so funny about Ali G.

In that karaoke bar in Rovaniemi, Col was confusing the hell out of me. To this day, I'm not sure if his version of Robbie Williams' 'Angel' was incredibly good or exceedingly bad. It was certainly surreal, seemingly never-ending and delivered with the intensity of someone who had actually written it. Well played, Colin.

Karaoke reared its head once more on our Scandinavian adventure—on the 'love boat' cruise from Helsinki to Stockholm. A group of us entered the top floor bar an hour before it shut at midnight. The audience was full of families, all of which seemed to have a fifteen year old daughter who wanted to be Mariah Carey. Each of these girls—God bless 'em—would stare nervously at the screen and deliver a sweet ballad to the supportive crowd. They didn't know what was about to hit them. I opened the account with a hair-raising version of Bon Jovi's 'You Give Love A Bad Name', before a rather bizarre announcement took place.

'And next,' said the guy on the mike in a thick Swedish accent, 'we have…Dirty Box. Is Dirty Box here?'

'Dirty Box', as it turned out, happened to be House, who proceeded to hold court—Sinatra-style—with a rendition of 'New York, New York'.

By now, our antics had inspired Marcus, a passenger whom we had never met until that moment, to come out of his shell. Tall, bald and smartly-dressed, Marcus strode centre stage and, instead of singing the song he had requested, proceeded to give a sermon on the evils of drugs. He was pointing at kids and telling them not to do it. This was somewhat ironic, given that he was as high as a kite. By now, the family atmosphere was in tatters, and the only thing that could bring it back was half a dozen of our group performing the B-52s' 'Love Shack'—with Marcus doing his best impression of a Mexican jumping bean.

The small Finnish town of Rovaniemi, though, was a real turning point for us on this trip. It was the place where, after five marathon days on the bus, we became human again. We were ready to peak at Rovaniemi, and it seems that at least half of our reminiscing about this twenty-two-day tour seems to concern the twelve-hour period we spent there. This was the place where we ditched those three gargoyles, where we met four Swedish glamours, where we heard Col sing 'Angel', and where House ran ten kilometres at 4.00 a.m. and didn't sleep at all.

This last story capped off a crazy night. I'll try to do it justice.

After our Swedish friends departed, the three of us were keen to kick on. We went to a nightclub, where we had varying degrees of success with the ladies. Col lucked out altogether, while House left the club early on with a more mature lady. I'll mention the girl I was chatting to, only because she said something very amusing to me at the end of the night. When I was leaving her to meet Col at a pre-arranged location outside the club, she asked me where I was going.

'To Helsinki,' I replied, 'to catch a boat.'

'Where to?' she asked.

'To England, and then I'm going back to Australia.' (It was nearing the end of my trip.)

'Australia?' she said. 'But it's so far!'

'You're right. It is.'

'Oh…' she sighed, before uttering in a pathetic tone, 'You idiot.'

'You idiot!' What is that all about? Apparently, I am an idiot because I come from a place that is a long way from her and, given that we had become so close over a period of thirty minutes, this was more than she could stand. She immediately sulked off, and I went to find Col.

In this task, I had absolutely no luck. Time had become a concept too challenging to contemplate, and Col had obviously left our appointed meeting place, believing he'd missed me. The gravity of the situation I was in suddenly dawned on me. It was 4.00 a.m., I was in a small town in the middle of Finland, I was on my own, I had nothing, I did not know the address of our camp site, I was quite pissed and becoming increasingly tired. I had to find Col.

At the same time, it turns out, the boys had met up and were looking for me. By sheer luck, a few minutes later I stumbled across them. House, by this time, had exchanged his first lady friend for a tall blonde who was riding around on her bike. House insists that he even took the bike for a spin round the town looking for me. Col was convinced that House had made no effort to locate me, and was vigorously challenging him on this very point when I found them. The last thing I wanted to do was stand in the middle of two old mates in order to prevent a barney, but that's what I found myself doing. Eventually, things calmed down. Col and I decided to get a taxi back to the camp site, while House informed us that he was going to accompany his new friend home.

After a couple of hours kip, Col and I rose and started to pack. The bus was rolling out at eight and I was on breakfast duty. Sometime after seven, in rocked House, and he had a funny tale to tell. Apparently, the blonde had come up with a cunning plan for them to make their way to her apartment. She would ride her bike, and House would run beside her. He claims, and I'm tempted to believe him, that he ran for fifty minutes. That would mean approximately ten kilometres—not bad for a bloke who was somewhat inebriated and wearing a pair of hard-soled shoes. Then, after some horizontal refreshment, he hopped into a taxi with little or no idea of where he was going. Beats me how he made it back, but he did, and was immediately back on the bus.

Doing away with the Nordkapp section of the tour (as I've previously suggested) would allow the group to skip straight across to Helsinki, and experience the charms of this superb city. From its distinctive railway station to its Reichstag (Parliament Building) to the memorials in Sibelius Park, it spoils the lover of architecture and design. And, gents, when you go to a nightclub, the 'ratio' (women to men) is outstanding. Centrally located on this occasion, we were able to take advantage of this and surround ourselves with more blonde beauties. What the hell were we doing in bloody Hammerfest?! One night in Helsinki and we were bound for the UK. We were gutted, but buoyed by one thing. For days, Bitches United had been spruiking about the fact that they were about to lose us and be joined by another group that was going on to Russia. They were sure that they'd find guys more to their liking within that group. On the night that we all met up for a farewell/welcome party, they were sorely disappointed. The five guys in the new group were, in the words of one of the little darlings, 'Poindexters'. How sweet it is!

Given that it took us three days to return to London, by bus and numerous ferries, I had plenty of time to make a list of some of the amusing Scandinavian words I had come across during the three weeks. The first thing one notices is their habit of including the word 'fart' in both common and proper nouns. 'Entry' and 'exit' are *infart* and *utfart*, and there's a Swedish town called *Middlefart*. Our bobsled in Norway was called *Sikker Fart*, obviously in honour of a regrettable incident in the past—no surprise, given the speed of the bugger. 'Out of order' is the rather harsh *slut*, a shock to any English-speaking woman hoping to buy a can from a Coke machine. The *Joker* supermarket chain, among others, sells some interesting products. Their version of Spam is *Bog*, there is a dog food called *Snog*, some tasty snacks by the name of *Cheesy Doodles*, and a chocolate treat (in appearance, dangerously close to a dog turd) called *Skum Bananer*. Sugar is the elegant *sukker*. Given that Australians sometimes refer to breasts as 'norks' and trousers as 'dacks', there was considerable mirth over a Swedish company called *Norks Dackservice*. My favourite, though, was in Finland. I didn't see what it was selling, but there was definitely a store in an arcade called *I Lust a Fagring*. Not to be left out, the Norwegians have named two of their towns *Hell* and *Bimbo*.

Although critical of several aspects of the tour, I got a great deal out of my three weeks in Scandinavia. I went partially for some natural scenery (and a break from castles, palaces and cathedrals) and was, on the whole, impressed. My photos of the fjords are like postcards, and the glacier was breathtaking, though I have since learned that comparable sights are on show in a far more accessible fashion (for Australians at least) in New Zealand. I'm glad I saw (and tasted) reindeer, but I'm mightily pissed off that the three times someone yelled 'Moose!' I was too slow to catch a glimpse. I guess I'm glad to have crossed the Arctic Circle. I'm definitely glad I was able to perv for my nation for three weeks solid. I'm glad to have honed my footy skills, the several half-hour road stops every day providing time for some invaluable kick-to-kick. And I'm glad to have met my two mates, House and Col, with whom I continue to reminisce about our travel-induced lunacy and our champion efforts at taking the piss.

Nine
New York:
Bright Lights, Big City...
and Big Hass!

I've seen a load of cool places in my time, but there are very few to which I would accord 'must see' status. London would be close, I guess, and probably Rome and Paris. Having been to New York, I now regard it as a 'must see' destination, particularly for those of us living in the western world. Let me explain why.

When I was a teenager, my friend read J.D. Salinger's *Catcher in the Rye* and raved about it for days. I always put it off, like one does with lots of things I suppose, but I made a mental note to one day read the book that made such an impact on my friend. That day came after my return from New York. I was supervising a test at my school in Canberra, bored out of my brain, when I noticed a copy of the aforementioned book at the front of the room. Having just finished a novel, there suddenly seemed no better time to take it home and delve into the adventures of young Holden Caulfield. After I read the final sentence a few days later, I reflected upon the reasons that *Catcher in the Rye* will remain a special book for me also. First, it is awesome in its own right—a beautifully crafted snapshot into the experiences of an American teenager at a turning point in his life, desperately in search of meaning and comfort. Secondly, and probably more importantly to me, it allowed me to feel at one with a book's setting to an unprecedented degree. Having been to New York a few weeks prior, I felt almost as though I was accompanying Holden—as he sat on a bench in Central Park, as he negotiated Grand Central Station, as he moved through the Village hunting for nightspots. The book was so alive for me. On returning to Australia, I have realised that the number of books, films and television programs set in New York is incredible. I find myself regularly pointing at the screen and saying, 'That's the Chrysler Building!' or 'There's Brooklyn Bridge!' Films like *Twelve Angry Men* and *Spiderman*, sitcoms like *Seinfeld* and *Friends*, are just a few that I've seen lately which somehow make more sense to me now. I don't think it's super-ficial—it's just that I feel as though I now understand (at least a little bit) New York City. The place is so prominent in our popular culture—you may as well get to know it.

New York epitomises so much. With its historic immigration depot at Ellis Island, its majestic and ever-watchful Statue of Liberty and its highly multicultural population, it epitomises the migrant experience. With its Stock Exchange on Wall Street and its scores of skyscrapers housing thousands of corporations, it epitomises the capitalist ideal. And with its millions of stores, big and small, its hot dog stands on every corner and the unique, no-fuss, straight-talking manner of those in constant pursuit of the holy 'buck', it epitomises the consumer culture…and, in many ways, the human spirit. It became clear to me, in just under a week in New York, that those who sought to destroy this spirit on 11 September 2001 never had a hope. New York exudes life, and seems to have an incredible hold on those who choose to make it their home. I'm glad to have returned to laid-back old Oz and its sleepy little bush capital (at least for now), but I'm glad I was able to gain something of an appreciation for the world's quintessential city.

After a year of intermittent travel, I was just about 'travelled out'. I had run out of energy and patience in Scandinavia, and New York was looming as an impediment to me getting home. Maybe I'd just chill out and save a bit of money, I thought. But when I actually got there, I felt the need to sightsee like a man possessed. How could I ever forgive myself if I went to New York and failed to see icons like the Empire State Building? Or Times Square? Or Wall Street?

These were places I had heard about since I was knee-high to a grasshopper. So, despite the fact that it was New York's third hottest week in a century, I got amongst it. I always prefer to sight-see on foot, and the incredible thing about New York's Manhattan Island (given that it is a 'new world' city) is that it is so compact you can actually do it. I reckon you could walk the length of Manhattan before lunch—if you were fit...and if you got up at about 6.00 a.m...and if you had a good supply of bandaids...

I walked almost the entire first day without stopping. My feet became so blistered that my pace was significantly reduced for the next two days, but I refused to accept defeat. In three days, I saw pretty much everything I'd ever heard of, discovering some unexpected treats along the way. The Metropolitan Museum of Art is a cracker, housing some gorgeous works by Matisse and that famous painting with ol' Georgie Washington crossing the Potomac. The Flatiron and Woolworth buildings are, for different reasons, extraordinary pieces of early twentieth century architecture. And, for replacing lost calories, I found Little Italy and Chinatown most satisfactory.

On Day Four, I took a three-hour boat cruise around Manhattan Island. This was recommended to me by a couple of friends and I hereby do the same to you. It allowed me to see everything I couldn't see by foot. The guide was a chap named Malarky Murray. How do I remember that? It could have something to do with the fact that he said it every two minutes, always as a postscript to one of his pieces of information, tall stories, pearls of wisdom or attempts at marriage guidance counselling.

'That there is the United Nations Building. I'm Malarky Murray.

'That there is where a man named Babe [Ruth] would one day change the face of world sport. I'm Malarky Murray.

'So I tell you, ladies and gentlemen, always treat your partner like your very best friend. I'm Malarky Murray.

'So if you've got some cash burning a hole in your pocket and you'd like to tip somebody with excessive generosity, just remember...I'm Malarky Murray.'

If I've been unkind to him, I really don't mean it. The guy could really spin a yarn. He was oozing with charisma and had a real star quality. I learned so much from him about New York and New Yorkers, about the turbulent history of the place, about its favourite sons and daughters, about Nine One One and the events that took place at Ground Zero, and about the most honourable ways to treat my fellow human beings. Malarky Murray knows an awful lot and, as a little extra, he is funny without trying. Ask for him by name—Malarky Murray.

It was great to see the dock on the Hudson from which the *Lusitania* departed (prior to being sunk by a German U-boat during World War I, killing one hundred and twenty-four Americans and contributing to the United States' decision to enter the war) and where the *Titanic* would have arrived (had it not sunk on its maiden voyage in 1912, killing more than fifteen hundred people). It was eerie to look at two of the World Trade Center buildings (there are several still standing) and imagine the Twin Towers behind them, rising to double their height. It was amusing to think that my first thought on seeing Yankee Stadium was that of *Seinfeld's* George Costanza. And it was a real eye-opener to see Ulysses S. Grant's tomb and have Malarky wax lyrical about one of America's most unlikely heroes.

On Day Five, I spent a fair chunk of time at and around Ground Zero. The gaping hole in the ground was being tidied up in readiness for the one year commemoration of the tragedy. I spent little time looking at the construction site itself, spending considerably more looking at the blue sky above, trying to imagine the sheer scale of the Towers. I tried to imagine the morning of the attack, everybody starting to go about their daily business. And I tried to imagine the planes hitting the buildings—a moment that words can't seem to express. I must say that the emotion of the events and their aftermath hit me less at the site than at the several memorials in surrounding streets—the messages and tributes at St Paul's Chapel and the badges from firefighters the world over at a nearby park. From an interest point of view, the greatest impact on me was made by the appearance of the buildings surrounding Ground Zero. I had believed, naively, that the Twin Towers had come straight down and that nearby buildings had miraculously escaped unscathed. In reality, several of them were left terribly burnt and scarred, and two of them were at this time wearing what can best be described as the world's largest sheaths. Who knows when they will be back to their original state? I also found out at the time that World Trade Center 7, noticeably shorter than the landmark Twin Towers, had collapsed shortly after it had been evacuated. I've since seen footage of this.

From reading all of the above you will probably agree that I deserved something of a break by Day Six—my last day in New York. I told my friends in Brooklyn, with whom I was staying, that I wouldn't be leaving the house on that particular day. I was going to spend my time preparing—both physically and mentally—for my marathon flight to Australia on the morrow. The best way to do that, I decided, was to watch a shitload of cable.

Before I go into my American cable television experience, I must mention the most exquisite culinary experience of my life, an experience that occurred during my visit to New York. My friends Joe, Stef and Rob suggested we all go out for dinner on my second last night in the country, and this led us to a Japanese restaurant called Nobu. From what I understand, there are two Nobu restaurants, and both are highly acclaimed. My guidebook said it was the second best restaurant(s) in New York, and I have no reason to doubt that. One of the premises is for celebrities and rich folk, a situation determined by the prices. The 'budget' Nobu allows no bookings and to get a table you just have to turn up and make a nuisance of yourself for between one and three hours.

The food, I was told, is the same. So, after making nuisances of ourselves for over an hour, we got in, and it was all worth it. The décor is classy, the service faultless and the food...to die for. All sorts of delectable little treats kept arriving at our table and I devoured them with as much decorum as I could feign. The highlight of the night, and, as a matter of fact, my entire eating career, was a chunk of cod which had been soaked in miso for (I can't remember so I'll make it up) six...no...nine months. It was unbelievable. Savoury and sweet collided that night at Nobu, and I swear I can still taste it. I immediately demanded to know whose suggestion the dish had been. Joe, it turned out, was the culprit. I told him that I was about to use a word to describe him that I did not 'bandy about loosely'. He was a 'genius'—a man fit to take his place alongside Galileo, da Vinci and Einstein. I doubt that I will ever top that taste sensation, and I doubt that I will ever pay more for a meal. US$65! This made the idea of spending the next day locked in Joe's apartment seem an even better one.

There are three types of men in this world—channel surfers, compulsive channel surfers and beyond-the-joke, sick-in-the-head channel surfers. I belong to the latter breed. And watching TV on a set as big as my house with a selection of more than one hundred channels was something akin to giving a drug addict $10,000 and allowing them to wander around Amsterdam for a day. Joe, I hope your remote's okay.

In more than ten hours of concentrated vegetating, by far the best program I found was a one-hour documentary on the history of the *Baywatch* television series. For the uneducated, *Baywatch* was, for the following reasons, something of a laughing stock among those with at least half a brain in Australia throughout the 1990s. First, every blonde bombshell in the show seemed to have either a past or a future in porn, a set of silicone tits heavy enough to inflict severe back or eye injury upon the wearer and hard enough to cut diamond, and an IQ lower than that of a red setter (but higher than that of their co-starring 'himbos'). This gave rise to a popular alternative title for the show: 'Babewatch'. Secondly, the network's promoters insisted on billing it as 'the world's most watched television program'—a farcical claim considering it was total shit. And thirdly, *Baywatch* starred David Hasselhoff.

David Hasselhoff—or Big Hass as I now like to call him—played a character called Mitch Buchanan. He basically strutted around all day, carrying an orange buoyancy device, showing off an increasingly flabby torso, and spurning the advances of hot chicks because he had lives to save. He and his ab-wielding sidekicks would save innocents from sharks, jellyfish, big waves (despite the fact that the surf was always flat) and, when these storylines eventually ran thin, he'd save them from bank robbers, terrorists and nuclear warheads. He wasn't shy with mouth-to-mouth and, in a fashion that undoubtedly left real-life paramedics shaking their heads, the victim invariably coughed up some water and recovered immediately. Half the time, the victim seemed to be Mitch's smart-arse son Hobie. I only watched *Baywatch* in the vain hope of seeing 'The Hobester' get his just desserts (a bit like *Jurassic Park* where I barracked for the dinosaur as it tried to eat that screaming bloody kid), but I didn't watch long enough to find out if he ever did.

I'd seen a little bit of David's work in the 1980s series *Knight Rider*, and I'd seen enough of him in *Baywatch* to realise that the guy had tickets on himself. But I had no idea of the extent of it until I watched this documentary. David Hasselhoff is the sort of guy that every David Hasselhoff dreams about. I don't mind blokes who are no good and know it. I've never had a problem with blokes who are good and know it. But I can't stand blokes who are no good but think they're bloody fantastic...except in this case! I find David Hasselhoff so funny that my interest in him is verging on something of an obsession. I've got all sorts of creative ideas. I'd like to overdub the entire eleven seasons of *Baywatch* with an absurd dialogue. I'd like to create a one-hour highlights package of some of Mitch's and Hass's best work and have it screened at primetime. One day, my friends, I will make my fortune out of David Hasselhoff.

Literally everything Dave said in the aforementioned documentary made him look like a complete schmuck. At one point, he claimed that he was kidding himself trying to be an actor (he didn't kid us!), and that his real passion was singing. Identifying musical comedy as his specialty, he modestly claimed that he had a 'really big voice'. A sadder indictment on the European pop scene than even the annual Eurovision Song Contest is that at one time in the 1990s, David Hasselhoff was the top-selling recording artist in continental Europe. (I'd like to tell you what he sang but I've absolutely no idea.) Not content with this, David tried in 1994 to make it big as a singer in the US by gambling on the production of a live pay-per-view concert. Sadly, minutes prior to the start of his concert, O.J. Simpson began his infamous dash for freedom in his white van, an event watched by an estimated ninety million viewers—all potential Hasselhoff converts! As it turned out, Big Hass only managed to pull 30 000 viewers (or the population of a large suburb), and his singing career on his home turf effectively bit the dust. Is it any wonder that, according to a news report, the poor bloke was hospitalised in 2002 for pouring the contents of his hotel mini-bar down his immaculately chiselled neck?

Numerous classic Hasselhoff blunders were presented that day on Channel 79. The piece de resistance, however, occurred when he was speaking about the idea of Avalon Beach in Sydney hosting *Baywatch's* ninth season (a plan later aborted due to a vigorous backlash by Avalon locals).

'If we shoot the show down here,' Hass announced, 'this could put Australia on the map!' This is rich—even for Hasselhoff. The suggestion that Australia has not already been put 'on the map' is almost as ridiculous (and insulting) as the idea that *Baywatch* is capable of performing such a deed. My American friend Joe, when told of this remark later that evening, asked me not to tell any Aussies about it because it would make Americans look bad. I told him it only made Hasselhoff look bad, and therefore I would be telling everybody I knew...and quite a few that I didn't know.

Recently, I saw a television promo for the Australian series *This Is Your Life*, hosted these days by Mike Munro. Though drowsy with fatigue at the time, I was certain that I saw an image of David Hasselhoff, before hearing that that particular week's show would be dedicated to an Australian pop star of the 1970s. I couldn't work it out, but thought the Hasselhoff bit must have been a snippet from an earlier episode, perhaps shot during his brief Avalon period. A couple of days later I was channel surfing when I came upon *This Is Your Life*. It was right at the end of the show and the singer Mark Holden was surrounded by a variety of people who had been important to him at some point in his life. And, wouldn't you know it, there was David Hasselhoff—putting Australia on the map right in front of my very eyes. Knowing that he would do or say something stupid, I dived for a nearby video cassette, but it was too late. The credits were rolling, the crowd was applauding and Hasselhoff was playing the goose—giving high fives to all and sundry, pumping his guns (biceps) and shooting imaginary bullets with both hands to everyone out there in TV Land, and all the time beaming with his pearly whites. I was so annoyed to have missed the majority of his injection into the program, but the next day I asked some of my students if they had seen it. A couple had.

'You should have heard him sing, sir!' one of them said.

'Why? What was he like?'

'He was hopeless,' a girl said, 'and he kept winking at the camera!'

He might have fooled the whole of Europe, but he's not fooling the youth of Australia, and he's certainly not fooling me. I wonder if he's ever considered a tilt at the Big Apple. As Frankie sang: 'If you can make it there...'

Ten
Miscellaneous Memories
from a Memorable Year

The first chapter of this book may have given you the impression that my time at Slothwick Skool was the most disheartening, infuriating and draining experience of my life. This is largely, but not strictly, true. There were certainly times in the attendance to my duties when I contemplated suicide...or homicide...or even genocide for that matter. These moments most commonly occurred when one or more morons insisted on trying to sabotage my class, or when one of the little ingrates blocked me in a passageway to say, 'G'day mate!' or during dinner-hall duty, when the dunces would see how far they could slide back down the evolutionary tree by pushing past me in their haste to stuff unhealthy amounts of white bread, sausages and deep-fried food into their halitosis-ridden gobs. But it was not all doom and gloom. I've already told you that I made friends on staff, and I did meet some (probably around a dozen) students that I actively liked. Further, on some occasions I actually had fun.

Slothwick's staffroom was its saving grace. I've never been to war, but I guess this room was like a bunker in that the ordeals taking place outside it served to bring its inhabitants closer together. Members of the hierarchy rarely appeared, and this fact gave us the freedom to explore reasons as to why our days and weeks seemed to be getting progressively more trying. When people cooled off, usually ten minutes into lunchtime, the stories emerged. This is my favourite.

Stan Marinda is a Namibian guy who teaches textiles. In my time at Slothwick, he was also responsible for the school's Personal Health and Safety Education (PHSE) program, a program condemning teachers to one hour per fortnight of compulsory pastoral care (otherwise known as babysitting) and a program that only he gave a damn about. As the school's first open evening approached, Stan took on the task of displaying around the school posters that students had produced, promoting various aspects of health and hygiene. 'Clean your teeth!' and 'Wear deodorant!' were some examples of the advice proffered. Just outside the staffroom appeared a poster that did not last long before being torn down by a highly offended female member of staff. Apparently, its creator had painted a naked woman and, above her head, inscribed the words, 'Wash Your Ming!' ('Minge' is a colloquial term for a woman's genitals, but, in true Slothwick fashion, it had been incorrectly spelt.) When objections to the poster were raised with a disgruntled Stan, it turned out that it had not simply evaded the detection of the censor (Stan). To this day, I'm not sure that he has any idea what was inappropriate about the poster. As a result of this incident, a deeply hurt Stan went into hibernation for two weeks, which was about as long as it took my mates and I to stop laughing. From then on, Stan was 'Ming the Merciless' and his PHSE program was the 'Ming Dynasty'.

After several months of fighting battles in class, I thought I'd try something that had worked for me in the past. Early in my teaching career I theorised that if I performed at school concerts, kids, as impressionable as they are, might think: 'Geez! He can sing, he's pretty cool, he's human!' At my school in Canberra, this never failed to have the desired result. It's like the kids unanimously decided: 'Mr Fowler's alright. We'll give him a break and take him off the list of people whose lives we intend to make a misery.' When the Slothwick Spring Concert rolled around, I was determined not to miss this opportunity. Teaming up with the best musician in the Sixth Form, I performed an acoustic version of Alex Lloyd's 'My Way Home' and, with a group of ex-students, played a heavier number by the band Stained. The generous applause that ensued made me believe that my cunning plan had worked. The next day, numerous kids approached me with comments such as, 'Good singing, Sir!' and 'You didn't tell us you could sing, Sir!' That was okay, but others hit me with the question: 'Sir, why did you sing?' I couldn't think of an answer then and I can't now. It's rare for me to be stuck for words, but that one nailed me. The next day they'd forgotten about the whole thing. I did not notice a skerrick of difference in the way they regarded me and I was back to square one, but I didn't lose my desire to get my hands on a microphone. When the PE staff asked me to fill the role of announcer at the regional athletics meet, I accepted with relish. At the end of the day, my PE colleagues were happy enough with my performance, but they made it clear to me that my style had been a little unorthodox. Apparently, previous announcers had stuck to providing essential information about the start times of track and field events. Strangely, they had fallen short of actually calling the races (I referred to students I didn't know as 'the blonde kid' or 'the kid in the blue'), of announcing odds on various events and of indulging in Barry White impersonations. Turkish made the mistake of promising to cough up 50p for every popular song title I mentioned and one pound for every Meatloaf song title—in context of course. (One of our colleagues hates Meatloaf with a passion that burns deep within every fibre of his being, hence the inspiration.) Talk about taking candy from a baby! How easy is it to use 'Bat Out Of Hell' and 'Two Out Of Three Ain't Bad' in the context of athletics? At one point I went for a Cyndi Lauper double: 'You know, I've been coming to these events for years, and "Time After Time" I've seen Slothwick athletes showing their "True Colours".' Thirteen pounds later and I was out the gate.

A couple of weeks later, things were shuffled so that I could perform the same duties at the Slothwick sports day. This was a very thoughtful going-away present, and I began to lick my lips at the thought of 'payback time'. Now the mongrels would have to listen to me, and I intended to make the most of it. I was at it all afternoon, though most of my remarks were about as subtle as a sledgehammer and therefore went straight over the heads of most. At one stage, some council employees called in to ask that we go easy on the microphone, as residents of nearby villages had complained about the noise. I thought this was a bit rich, considering it was the middle of the day, but I knew the 'fun police' were never far away in the UK.

'They must be used to this,' I said, defending myself. 'These sorts of events take place all the time.'

'Yes,' they replied, 'but usually the announcers don't talk the whole day without a break.' I think it was my excitable race-calling (Darrel Eastlake-style) which caused the problem. This year, I'm told, they selected the considerably more reserved Turkish to do the job. The thinking was that he wouldn't 'yak on all day'.

The fun police were also in evidence at Edgbaston County Cricket Ground in Birmingham, the scene of the Second Test between England and Sri Lanka. I was one of three teachers who accompanied about fifty kids to the first day's play. Plenty of wickets fell that day (mostly Sri Lankan), so the crowd was upbeat. I only had a few weeks to go in the UK and I decided to let my hair down. By the final session, we had the kids (some of whom were likeable) chanting, singing, doing the Mexican wave and starting conga lines. It was at this point that the fun police (security officers) made their mark. Perceived as the ringleader, I was pulled aside by one of them (whose walkie-talkie was, I believe, loaded) and told that by being on our feet we were blocking the view of people behind us. It was after 6.00 p.m. and, as a glance behind me confirmed, there was nobody left in the stand. As I began to assert this point, I was interrupted by the students' rendition of 'Fowler's going to the Big House' ('He's going down, he's going down...'). This, along with my relentless bagging of England 'pace' bowler Andy Caddick (in the absence of the perennial 'bunny' Alan Mullally), was clearly enough to guarantee anyone temporary hero-status at Slothwick. They picked me up and chaired me out of the ground, pausing only once so that I could shake the hand of former Australian Test cricketer Michael Slater, who had been doing some commentary work. 'G'day Slats,' I said to a man with no idea what was going on. 'Glenn Fowler, Slothwick Skool.' You've got to fly the flag once in a while.

The other daytrip for me in the summer term was with the History staff and ninety Year 9 students to the World War I battle-fields, cemeteries and memorials in Belgium. This trip alternates with a Somme tour, and I was a little disappointed that I'd missed that opportunity, as I haven't yet made it to the Somme to see the grave of a relative. Although I'd been to Ypres in Belgium before, I wasn't to be disappointed by the day's itinerary, as it was almost totally different from the one I'd followed in 1997. The highlights for me were the Langemarck German Cemetery (its flat black plaques creating a very different and more eerie atmosphere from that engendered by the crisp white headstones in British Commonwealth war cemeteries), Passchendaele Ridge (where Australian soldiers made extraordinary progress at the expense of one death for every three centimetres of ground gained, only to see the village retaken by the Germans within a week), and watching the ignoramuses (or is it ignorami?) from Slothwick impose them-selves on the whole scene. To their credit, and under the threat of death, they resisted the temptation to run between the headstones (like we saw one London school doing), but the task of maintain-ing a sombre and reflective demeanour was often beyond them. I could understand their excitement. This wasn't Stevenage, and it wasn't Tenerife or Ibiza[12]—this was somewhere completely differ-ent. Hence, the cameras worked overtime, though rarely on any of the sights. I can picture their parents being shown the photos:

[12] A bit like Bali or Great Keppel for Australians, only less classy.

'Here's one of me. Here's another one of me. Here's one of me with Amy. Here's one of me with Sarah doing the bunny ears behind my head. Here's one of me giggling in front of a grave. Here's one of me standing in a trench with my arms outstretched in unbridled jubilation with a grinning face that would be more appropriate at Disneyland. Here's one of Bradley putting dog poos into my mouth...'

I spent much of the day transfixed by this absurd behaviour and laughing with Vaughan about it. Maybe one day, in several years time, the significance of what they saw will have an impact on them.

In 1997, after spending twenty-seven days driving around England, Wales and Scotland in a hire car, I felt fairly content that I'd seen most of what there is to see. The one exception was the West Country of England—specifically the counties of Devon and Cornwall—and I was determined to have a look this time around. The May Bank Holiday weekend provided the excuse. I, along with my three travel companions, stopped at a quiet little pub in Somerset to watch my newly beloved Arsenal win the FA Cup Final. During the half-time break, I fell into a discussion with one of the locals about the various groups of football (soccer) supporters around the UK. He claimed that the racist elements up north are 'not that bad', before informing me that his hometown, Bradford, has been 'taken over by Pakis'. He went on to talk about Australian Aborigines before checking that he hadn't offended my Indian-Canadian friend, whom he of course believed was Aboriginal.

I'm glad that I made the effort to get to these parts of England. Tintagel, the legendary seat of King Arthur's Court, is spectacular, and the coastal villages of St Ives, Polperro and Mousehole (pronounced Mouzal) are beautiful. The architecture is like nothing else in England, as are the accents, which sounded more Irish than English to me (a statement which would undoubtedly get me into a fight). Cornwall is the home of the pasty and Devon the home of clotted cream ice-cream, and I made sure I tried both. They were good, baby.

There were only a couple of downers. I had heard good things about the village of Clovelly in Devon. On arriving, though, we discovered that we would have to pay to get *in* to the village! The bearer of this news was a condescending ponce, about seven feet in height, who was obviously doing collections for his mater and pater.

'Sorry mate,' I said. 'Isn't this a village?'

'It is,' he replied, 'and a privately-owned one.' Why one should have to spend money for the privilege of spending more money, I will never know. His advances on our wallets were promptly spurned and we were on our way—out of principle more than anything else. The second downer was experiencing the notorious Bank Holiday traffic on the way home. Our lowest ebb was sitting in one spot for over an hour listening to countless repetitions of that bloody Holly Valance song. It was like being 'Kiss Kissed' to death.

Part of my rationale for gallivanting around Europe for a year was that, after a very late start in life, I had a lot of partying to get out of my system. Mission accomplished—I've quietened down a fair bit now as I contemplate marriage, fatherhood and a mortgage, and I've even considered becoming a monk.[13] I had some fantastic weekends during my year away. One that springs to mind is that of my Australian friend Ed's thirtieth birthday bash (October 2001) at his and his wife Merren's flat in London. Not only did I procure my highly prized mullet wig; I witnessed from the balcony a scene that I will never forget. One guest, dressed as Darth Vader, went downstairs to lie on the bonnet of an empty police car, whose occupants had gone into a flat to investigate the setting off of an alarm. Ed, dressed as Superman, discovered that the handbrake had not been applied and thought the situation would be improved by him pushing the car and Darth (who was

[13] Outright lie.

still spreadeagled on the car) along the road. The bobby emerged and, incredibly to us, couldn't see the funny side. Ed, a lawyer, and capable of talking his way out of Death Row, was able to put the officer's mind at ease and the party continued.

On 26 January 2002, Ed and Merren threw an Australia Day party, and a lot of Aussies turned up. My good mate Dominic (the one who was married in Chile) was in town 'on business' and, just before the party started, showed off a hat that he had bought for his wife Ali. Scott, another Australian holidaying in the UK, tried on the hat for a lark, only to discover that in doing so he had transformed himself into Jay Kay, the front man for Jamiroquai. The likeness was uncanny. So, we hatched a plan. A couple of hours into the party, a few of us started to spread the word that Jay Kay would be turning up, as he was a close friend of ours. A little while later, Scott ducked out, only to reappear as Jay Kay—resplendent in his funky hat and a large overcoat. We ushered him into a dark corner where we acted aloof and really cool for a while, and then, after customary farewell embraces, he left. I am only telling you this story because one of the couples at the party left before we came clean, and apparently continue to tell people that they went to a party with Jay Kay. I do love practical jokes—harmless ones. I'm prepared to admit that the following one was right on the borderline. In fact, I'm wincing now as I think about it.

In May 2001, I attended a conference for educators in Japan, at which there were representatives from seventeen nations. The situation I found myself in was slightly farcical really. Out of more than eighty people, I was the youngest by at least ten years, and about the only one who was a standard teacher. Most were deputy principals, principals and even regional directors. Even the story of how I got to go is a farce. A departmental fax found its way on to my desk at work one day. Having been to China the year before on a teacher's tour, I didn't think I could justify—or swindle—another trip to Asia. I put the fax in the bin, then pulled it out and called the advertised number. The following conversation took place:

'Hi. How much does the trip to Japan cost?'

'Nothing—it's all paid for.'

'Really? How many people have applied?'

'None—you're the first.'

'When do applications close?'

'Tomorrow.'

I couldn't believe it. One scribbled application later, and I was Japan-bound. I'll need to make a conscious effort to remember that story every time I feel like the world is against me.

When we arrived in Tokyo, they gave each of us A$1000 to spend. There was very little to spend it on—five-star accommodation was fully paid for, as were the frequent banquets. It was lucky, because Japan is bloody expensive. Other than that, I reckon I could live in Japan—for a while. The people are impeccably polite and friendly, the food is divine and the culture is highly sophisticated. Yet, it was probably the least sophisticated element—the Sumo wrestling—that was the highlight for me. Those guys are so fast...so powerful...so fat.

I struck up a friendship with a couple of Kiwis when I was in Japan. One night, we were throwing around ideas for pranks that we could play on our lovably fastidious chaperone and guide, Nori (Japanese for 'seaweed'). I came up with one idea and, having made the suggestion, felt bound to execute it. The next day, we were to ride the famous bullet train. From memory, this mad thing goes at between three hundred and four hundred kilometres per hour. (Apparently, it is common for stressed-out students to meet their maker by flinging themselves into its path.) When it pulls up at a station (which occurs rarely), it stops for just under a minute, before tearing off again. Nori was frantic with worry about our large group getting on the train within the allotted time. His insistence on us lining up in twos (primary school style) was the result of a previous experience in which a guy had strayed from the group to take a photo and was inadvertently left behind. We knew that on the final section of our return to Tokyo, there was only one stop. It was there that we would strike.

As the train pulled up, I steeled myself, then rose to my feet, grabbed my small backpack and left the train. Bizarrely, nobody seemed to notice (except my giggling partners-in-crime) until I was on the platform, making my way nonchalantly past the train. A Singaporean lady in our group finally noticed me and screamed: 'What is he doing?' It was then that Nori shat himself. Leaping to his feet, he instinctively grabbed his jacket and valuables from the rack above (I think he might have actually rehearsed this contingency plan) and made his way to the door. He didn't get that far—my friends told him to look around and he saw me. I was ba ҫ in the carriage, having re-entered from the back. Nori eventually talked fondly of the ruse and of us, but at the time, the strain of seeing his career flash before his eyes caused him to break into a cold sweat.

In this chapter, I've mentioned my friends Ed and Merren a couple of times. It would not be right, though, to do so without linking them to sport. The pair is thoroughly obsessed with it and, if they're not playing, they're generally spectating—cricket, basketball, rugby, Aussie Rules, soccer—you name it. I love the story of their engagement, which took place several years ago. Ed's plan was as follows. He would ask Merren to join him in an evening stroll down to the beach from their apartment at Bondi in Sydney. Here, he would produce from his pocket a ring and from his bag a bottle of champagne to toast her acceptance. They would then return to their apartment where, Cheezels[14] at the ready, they would watch the Australian Socceroos dispose of the

---

[14] A cheese-flavoured snack food.

struggling Iran at the Melbourne Cricket Ground to waltz into their first World Cup Finals for twenty-four years. Yes, that's right—Ed was going for the big double. The first part of the plan was executed with military precision and the second part seemed to be heading the same way, but, as many of you will have realised already, things were about to go horribly wrong. At 2–0 up and looking the goods, the Socceroos conceded two late goals to be bundled out on a count back. So Ed, on what should have been the happiest night of his life, went to sleep muttering: 'Fuck! Fuck! This is the worst fucking night of my miserable life!'

Merren is an accomplished basketballer and, having played at the highest level in Australia, had no trouble slotting into a team in the somewhat weaker British League. But as good as she is, Merren seemed to be significantly less well known within British basketball circles than her husband Ed—not bad for someone who wasn't even playing. What brought Ed such notoriety was his habit of mouthing off on the sideline. I know this because he invited me to join him in the stands, and the fact that I ended up joining him on two occasions indicates that I did not disapprove of his antics. Actually, I felt obliged to contribute, and together we reached new heights of smart-arsery.

Turning up at a West London gym in the early afternoon with a six pack of beer immediately had us on the fun police radar. When we were told we couldn't drink inside the stadium, we drank outside the stadium; watching the girls warm up through the large glass windows, and laughing at how unsophisticated we must have looked. By tip-off time, we had found our seats, right in the middle of everyone (well, the thirty or so who were there). Merren's team had the rather ridiculous name of Spelthorne, and the idea was to amplify the ridiculousness of this word by getting it wrong—in a different way—every time we shouted it out. 'Spinklehempelstead' and 'Spoofhorn' were among our favourites. First-naming the coaches ('Come on Terry, back to basics, huh!')

and the opposition ('You're better than that, Georgia!') brought chuckles. (We'd got hold of the program, you see.) Then there was the old chestnut—abusing the referees—an assignment for which Ed was exceedingly qualified. At one point, the bald ref found himself on the end of this stinging rebuke from the master: 'Hey Curly! You wouldn't know a foul if it laid an egg!' And the thing is, Ed does know fouls. He's a fairly handy player himself, and he has a sound technical knowledge of the game. I saw an opportunity to put this to good effect and, after some consultation, was able to offer all sorts of constructive criticism to the girls. 'Box out!' (genuine), 'Box in' (fabricated), 'Work hard on the paint' (courtesy of watching some American basketball on the TV) and 'Drive and dish' (just sounds good) were all pieces of advice offered—and ignored. In the end, the crowd started to see us as a pair of lovable rogues, and we all left in good spirits.

I'd like to tell you about the time in May 2002, when I attempted to pack three huge nights into one weekend. The first night consisted of a dinner in London, where I was introduced to a nice guy called Al whom I could tell was pretty switched on. Turned out he was switched on enough to be earning more money in a fortnight than I do in a year. I was conned into a night on the sauce, and Al took Dom and I to a club so cool that it didn't even have a name. He winked at some bald-headed, murderous-looking chap who let us in. I thought I'd better get Al a drink, but he wouldn't have it. I watched him pay two hundred pounds (over five hundred Australian dollars) for a bottle of champagne, realising that I was rather out of my depth. How do you shout someone a beer after that? For an hour and a half, the bottle sat in the middle of the bar—and nobody stole it! This was truly a classy establishment. I didn't have the heart to tell him that I wouldn't know the difference between a two hundred-pound bottle and a five-pound bottle. To be honest, I don't think he would have cared. He was too busy fighting off women.

The next night, Saturday, Dom and I headed off to School Disco (not *a* school disco, but School Disco, as in schooldisco.com). The concept has just arrived in Sydney, but for those of you who don't know the score, I'll explain briefly. You dress in school uniform (mandatory), you drink heavily while standing in line to get in (to avoid needing too many pricey drinks inside), you get frisk searched (even if you don't request it), you enter an enormous cavern (room), you pay a fortune for drinks (unless you're Al, then it's a pittance), you dance to shitty 1980s music, and you enjoy the company of girls (if you're a guy) who, for some inexplicable reason, generally fulfil the criteria of being attractive *and* lacking in inhibition. I was pleasantly surprised the first time I had my bottom grabbed, and it was to happen numerous times thereafter (and usually by females!). I then cottoned on to a wonderful game. Make your mate (in this case the blissfully unaware Dominic) walk in front of you through the throng, reach around him and grab a peach, and sit back and watch the reaction. The thing is, though, at School Disco it is invariably quite okay. I guess the rule is: If you're not up for it, don't go. Fair enough. The night ended with Dom and myself lining up in a kebab joint asking those who had just received their food if they were 'going to eat that'. We always were easily amused.

Sunday night I went to Brixton Academy to see Tool, one of my favourite bands. They were undoubtedly good, but I was too fatigued to notice. I did the unthinkable and left early. I thought there might be some delays making my way home to Hertfordshire. Two nights earlier, five people had died when a train derailed and struck the platform at Potters Bar, and this was on my line. The British really must do something about their rail system.

Talking of great parties, have you heard about a place in North London called The Church? This is another unique experience. This converted warehouse only opens its doors between 12 noon and 3.30 p.m. on a Sunday, and the aim is to pack in as much fun as possible in a short time. It's not difficult. There are comedians, strippers (male or female—it's potluck), beers in bags of three and wonderfully appropriate music—geared to the twenty to thirty-five set, and much of it Australian. They play Midnight Oil, INXS, ACDC and things like 'Sweet Home Alabama'. The idea for The Church was conceived by Aussies and Kiwis, who now manage the place. It attracts a high proportion of ex-pats, and there is never any trouble on account of the fact that the Maori bouncers would only need to look at you to make the brown undies a necessity. In terms of party times, this is quality, not quantity. Everyone is pumped and the place just rocks. There is an incredible sense of unity, perhaps because people feel that they are with their own kind in a foreign land, and the music reinforces this. At the very early closing time, some kick on in nearby pubs, while others return home to prepare for work on the Monday.

I'll wind up this chapter with one last story about my bungling sidekicks of Hungary fame. The day I went to The Church, I decided to top off the afternoon by joining a couple of friends over the road at a pub called (get ready to wince) The Backpackers. Mike and Turkish decided against an extension to their day and went to nearby Kings Cross Station to catch different trains home. It was 4.00 p.m. when I arrived at the pub. I left at 6.45 p.m. and was through the front door of my house at 7.30. A quick wee and it was off to bed. The next day, as we sat in the staffroom looking a little worse for wear, the three of us compared times at which we had arrived home. It was revealed, to my astonishment, that I was the first to arrive home.

'What the hell happened to you freaks?' I politely asked. The stories unfolded.

Mike boarded his train and, as it left the station for the twenty-minute journey to his stop, began to feel sleepy. Asking the woman beside him if she wouldn't mind waking him at Welwyn

Garden City, he drifted off into Noddy Land. Some time later, he was awoken by the sensation of the train hitting the platform. Looking out, he saw that he was back at Kings Cross Station and, glancing at his watch, he noticed that it was almost 7.00 p.m. It seems he had travelled all the way to Cambridge (almost one and a half hours away) and all the way back. His fellow traveller had failed to wake him, as had any train conductors. Knowing how hard he is to wake, however, I'm not surprised. He is the sort of guy who could sleep on a camel ride.

Turkish had a different tale to tell, and a miserable one at that. The initial movement of the train clearly got all his juices flowing—in the wrong place and at the wrong time. Within seconds of the train departing, he found himself locked in a desperate battle with his bladder. Too drunk to locate a toilet, he was suddenly struck by a brilliant idea. He would go up to the front of the train, where nobody ever sits, and he would pass water behind the driver's door. He sprang into action and got as far as undoing his fly, before being jolted by a loud thumping on the other side of the driver's door, followed by an instruction. 'Fuck off!', I think, was the command. Scurrying away, he realised that there was only one option left to him. He would have to get off the train. The next stop was lonely Potters Bar and he was up against a lamp pole like a flash. Relieved, he wandered down the platform to check the timetable. It was bloody cold, so he hoped the next train wouldn't be too long. Now if I was to pick one of my mates who would have the rotten luck of standing on a deserted platform at Potters Bar, shivering in his boots, gradually sobering up and dreading the thought of teaching all day with a hangover…for a period of ONE HOUR AND TEN MINUTES, who would that be? Don't go changing Turkish—you are far too funny.

Eleven
Britain:
My Report Card on the Poms

I've been to Britain twice now, and I must say that the feeling I get when I go there is quite unique. When I go for a third time, I'll undoubtedly feel different again. It will be like a mini-homecoming—returning to the place where I lived for twelve months. That makes sense, but it doesn't explain the way I felt when I arrived in Britain the first two times. Even when I'd never been there, it felt like I was *returning*. It's strange that I felt that way, because as an Australian one is bombarded with the culture of both Britain *and* America, yet I did not feel anything like the same way when I visited the US. It seems my British blood runs far deeper than I had realised. I'm not saying I fitted straight in—far from it—but a lot was familiar to me: phrases people used, the TV shows they watched, the jokes they found funny, the names of places, the landmarks, the institutions. I reckon there is definitely some strange, indefinable attachment that Australians (at least if they are of British stock) have for Britain. Any thoughts?

Almost a year since I left the place, there are still things I miss about Britain.

As a history teacher, I relish being surrounded by really old stuff. I love old buildings, old streets, old cemeteries, old burial mounds, old castles, old palaces and old churches. In Britain and Europe, one is constantly reminded that one is a part of history— and I really love that. Most things are so new here in Australia that we rarely get that feeling. Our old is like their new. I love the way old buildings look, the way they get better with age, the way they look as though they will be there forever. It really is true— they just don't make 'em like they used to.

London is a brilliant city and I miss not being close to it. For the historian, it is a veritable treasure chest. I took countless daytrips to the Imperial War Museum, to the Cabinet War Rooms, to the British Museum, to the galleries. And the nightlife is great too—pubs, clubs, places to eat. One is constantly surrounded by people on the move. The place is so old, yet so *alive*.

I miss British pubs…boy, do I miss the pubs. Good pubs are like rocking horse shit in Canberra, a fact that I am reminded of almost every weekend. In my little English town of Hitchin, a town of 30 000 people, there are more than thirty pubs—most of them good, and almost all having something different to offer. The names are cool too—The Sir John Barleycorn, The Tut 'n' Shive, The Cock (named after Chuck Norris apparently). I love the fact that in Britain, you can walk down the street, think to yourself: 'You know, I could really do with a drink…and some lunch' and know that there is an eighty per cent chance[15] of the first pub you walk into being cosy, full of character and serving good honest fare. One gripe I had was that they sell terrible lagers—Carling (local piss), Kronenberg (French piss) and bloody Fosters (I still don't know how they get the cat to squat over the bottle). I missed my premium Aussie lagers, that's for sure (and I will happily do any promotional work in this regard). When I first arrived in England I drank ales and bitters, but I got tired of my friends saying: 'And would you like to borrow a backgammon set with that?' (It turns out these are what old people drink.)

Some of these pubs, especially the country ones, have been in the one family for generations, and the walls and shelves are covered with fascinating memorabilia. It's like you've stumbled into the family's living room and you are free to wander around and have a stickybeak. There's always at least one old bloke sitting there—a great uncle or something—who looks like he hasn't

[15] My friend Chris once told me that 86.9 per cent of statistics are made up on the spot.

moved since he last went to the toilet in 1973. If you can decode his accent, there's sure to be a pearl of wisdom just below the surface—or a comment that seems unrelated to anything you've ever heard in your life, but which prompts you to agree whole-heartedly. And lots of these places house a friendly dog. (In France, these tend to be in restaurants as well.)

I'd love to have a 'local'. In Canberra, the closest thing to a half-decent pub is kilometres away. But in Hitchin, the best pub in town, Molly Malone's, was less than a stone's throw from my front door (and just far enough away for us not to hear its imbibed patrons if we didn't want to). Molly's was always good for a couple of Friday night drinks, and on Sunday night, 'Trotsky' the barman would become Trotsky the quizmaster. Not being British was a huge disadvantage in these affairs and my Canadian flat-mates and I were generally put to the sword. We had a few laughs though. One night, we chose 'The Aliens' as our team name, to reflect our foreign origins. At the end of the quiz, Trotsky would throw the names of every team who failed to finish in the top three into a hat, and the team he picked out would take home a bottle of wine. On this particular night, 'The ALLENS!' brought home the bickies. What sort of team name is 'The Allens'? Well, it is the name we asked the entire pub to toast!

The next closest pub to our house, about one hundred and fifty metres up the road, was an establishment called The Woolpack. This is the most obvious exception to every generalisation I previously made about the charm of British pubs. In our first week in Hitchin, Grace and I thought we'd duck in for some lunch. Now I'm telling you, I have never done a faster and smoother one-hundred-and-eighty-degree turn in my life. For a start, the place smelt to high heaven of marijuana—it nearly knocked us off our feet. And through the smoke, I could just make out a gang of Rastas, who were clearly involved in a drug deal and looked at us as if to say: 'You got somewhere to be?' I could not see any beer taps or chairs and I rated my chances of procuring a light meal as negligible. We were in there for about one and a half seconds. A few months later, the police shut The Woolpack down, and it stayed that way until I left. From what I understand, the authorities had always known that dope was being sold in the place (you wouldn't need to be Einstein), but that at least it was contained in the one area. I take it the dealers started to push the boundaries and sell other substances also. Anyone who had ever bought dope in England seemed to know about The Woolpack. When people heard I was from Hitchin, they'd often ask me if I'd been there. I met one English guy in Greece that said he always bought his gear from The Woolpack. The place is legendary, mon. For me, it was legendary because of the story I heard about the laundry across the road—a laundry I used several times before hearing this story. Apparently, the large dent in one of the industrial washing machines was caused by a drugged-to-the-eyeballs Woolpack patron taking to it with a machete. Fair enough—perhaps his favourite shirt had shrunk.

Another thing the Poms do well is the supermarket. I always went to Sainsbury's in Hitchin and, for the first time in my life, enjoyed shopping for food. (No, I'm not on their payroll...yet.) They had all sorts of options—ten different types of bagel, thirty different types of yoghurt, a wide selection of low-fat, ready-made meals, quality sushi and some excellent Australian wines that are not easy to find in Australia. (How am I going, Sainsbury's?) Further, every single British food item, without fail, lists the fat percentage of the product. This fact, along with the excellence of their supermarkets, is ironic, given that many of the Poms I met had absolutely no idea how to eat. I'll deal with this point later in the chapter. But one thing I would like to raise now is the British policy of making you put the food in the bags yourself.

Australian checkout attendants, from a standing position, place the items in a bag for you as they ring them up. Their British counterparts sit, ring up the items and chuck them on the table.

During the time you are at the checkout, you, unlike them who do next to nothing, are under enormous pressure. Almost simultaneously, you need to find the money in your wallet, check and put away your change, hand over your Sainsbury's reward card, take your receipt, and put all of your items into plastic bags clearly designed by Bastards Incorporated. And all this under the steely glare of a line of increasingly impatient shoppers who, due to store policy I presume, do not have the first of their items rung up until you have totally cleared the area. It's a bit like a pit stop in Formula 1. When I'm reincarnated, I'd like to work on the checkout at Sainsbury's. What a cakewalk!

As you grow older and wiser and travel around a bit, you start to realise that most of the generalisations and stereotypes you hear about as a kid are unreliable. You start to see the complexity of things and realise that there are two sides to every coin. You start to realise that people are far more similar than they are different, and that everyone deserves to be given the benefit of the doubt— at least initially.

There are only two stereotypes that I have found will hold true one hundred per cent of the time:

1. Old people cannot drive. I know I'm going to upset a few people with this one, but I'm going to stick to my guns. Old people on the road have lost all ability to accelerate up to the speed limit, to read the flow of traffic, to be perceptive to the needs of those around them, and to drive to avoid red lights. I've always found it ironic that those with the least time left on the earth act as though they have all the time in the world. I love that skit I once saw on a comedy show where a crack team of old people are sent out to get in people's way and to slow them down when they're in a hurry— in banks, in supermarkets and on the road. And they are all dressed in lawn bowling attire.

2. All police spokespeople speak the same. You know what I'm talking about. 'Today, at 2.36 p.m., four persons were apprehended leaving the scene of an alle-ged hold-up…a total of no persons became deceased as a result of the alle-ged shooting, though a total of two persons were alle-gedly injured…blah blah blah…' I'd like to meet the guy who trained them all in this monotonous way of speaking—the famous 'Man with No Emotion'. He must be a real livewire. I wonder if he hosts parties?

The reason I wanted to present these two examples is to make it abundantly clear that the generalisations I am about to make about the British are by no means true *all* of the time, and they are by no means true of *all* British people. I present to you the norms, not the exceptions.

1. The British make sure that nothing is easy.

I was introduced to this phenomenon in the first few days of my stay. Until the three of us were able to get into the house we intended to rent, we 'dossed' (stayed with) Kevin's previous flatmates at their house in the town of Cheshunt. One night I asked one of them how she had found the UK in the year that she had been here.

'It's been okay, but…' and she paused, '…you don't know what it's like, do you?'

'What do you mean?' I asked, in all my naivety.

'Nothing is easy,' she said, before providing numerous examples of how tough it was to get things done.

I would often reflect on these prophetic words in my year away. In fact, I had cause to reflect on them two days later.

Five days we had waited for the estate agents to run checks on us and, after four nights staying with people we didn't know and one night in an expensive (by our standards) hotel in Stevenage, my patience had evaporated. It was always a case of 'probably tomorrow'. And they weren't fooling me—I know that Interpol is capable of running quicker checks than that.

So on the evening of the fifth day, we collected all our stuff and caught the train into Hitchin. We fronted up to the estate agent's shop and told them that we would be camping on the doorstep if they didn't let us into the house. Funny, but we had the keys in less than an hour.

Within a week, I was making inquiries as to how to obtain a National Insurance number. This is like a Medicare number and, although I was subsequently unable to discern any practical difference between having one or not, it was apparently essential. After being led on a telephonic wild goose chase, I eventually spoke to a lady from the Stevenage branch of the Department of Delays, Red Tape and Incompetence. She told me that I would need to apply in person for this number, that I would need to make an appointment, that this appointment would have to be before 3.00 p.m. on a weekday (highly convenient for a teacher) and that their first available appointment was in two months time. Not perturbed, I checked my school timetable and found an afternoon where I had a lesson off and therefore I could do it. I told the Deputy Head of Slothwick, out of politeness, that I would be attending a vital appointment that particular afternoon—not that I figured it was any of his business, but just in case he found the need on that day to book me for 'cover'[16]—and guess what? They made me fill out a bloody form!

[16] I can't believe that it has taken me more than ten chapters to have my first whinge about this system. 'Cover' was the bane of my existence at Slothwick. I've already told you that I taught two hundred and sixty kids across ten classes. What I didn't tell you was that I had only eight hours of non-teaching time per fortnight. And what I also didn't tell you was that in those non-teaching lines, I could, without any notice at all, be used to cover my sick colleagues. This was not only grossly inconvenient if one had preparation planned in those times, but grossly unfair. Unlike others, I (as an international 'supply' teacher) was being paid by the day and I couldn't afford to be sick. Even when I was on my deathbed (and I occasionally was, as I struggled to cope with flu strains to which I had no immunity) I made it into work. In other words, NOBODY WAS COVERING ME! I bitched about this quietly for a while, before gaining myself quite a reputation for emitting loud and terrible obscenities when my daily check of the 'cover sheet' bore bad tidings.

So, in two months time, I, along with my seven forms of ID, fronted up to the appointment. I was ushered into a tiny office where I produced payslips, bank balances, electricity bills, dental records, last will and testament, Hellfire Club membership card, and so on. The woman made me sign each of the thirty pages in some document, before disappearing for fifteen minutes. When she came back, she produced page eighteen of this document, on which my signature had been deemed unacceptable—I think the 'G' was a little larger than it was on the others. I placated her and she disappeared for another fifteen minutes. When she returned, she told me that I would be receiving my National Insurance Number in the mail—sometime in the next three months. It took four.

In Chapter Ten, I mentioned the dangers posed by the inadequate upkeep of the British rail system. Crashes are not an uncommon occurrence and seem to make it into the news periodically. Although one's chances of being involved in something like that are miniscule, one's chances of being inconvenienced by British trains are enormous. Several times, just when I needed it least, I would turn up to train stations to be told that the trains had stopped running for the day (usually due to technical problems or driver shortages) and that I would need to wait for the next bus. The British themselves tend to deal with this situation by keeping the quintessential 'stiff upper lip', but you can generally see them fuming inside. On one occasion, however, coming home from London late at night and going round the world on one of these antiquated buses, I was privileged to witness some champagne comedy. I remember very little of the actual dialogue that took place (and I have promised myself that in future I will always arm myself with a tape recorder), but it basically involved a couple of cockneys positively hanging it on this muddle-headed old bus driver in a light-hearted fashion. The driver seemed to be in regular contact with other drivers as they sought to ferry home thousands of people who would normally have caught trains. Each time his mobile phone rang, these blokes would pretend to be the voice on the other end of the phone. 'Hello darling, when will you be home?' they would say in their best fishwife voice, or 'Don't crash now love, and kill all those nice people.' The driver, being considerably more sober than they were, did not find it as hilarious.

The London Underground (or 'The Tube') is fantastic when it works. You can get from one side of London to the other in a matter of minutes and it is very simple to negotiate your way around. The problem is, as any commuter will tell you, that stuff-ups are as common on the Tube as they are on the trains. I remember one time when I was pushed up against smelly people at the end of a long day, in oppressive heat, just praying (for the first time ever) for the bloody thing to start moving. I've no idea how a claustrophobic person could have got through it. Nothing could have cheered me up on that particular occasion, but in less revolting circumstances it is possible to be entertained by the dry wit of the drivers over the microphone. There are websites devoted to their quips. My favourite is:

'I apologise for the delay leaving the station, ladies and gentle-men. This is due to a passenger masturbating on the train at Edgware Road. Someone has activated the alarm and he is being removed from the train.'

The realisation that these men are human is always refreshing.

It's not just government agencies and public utilities that are plagued by preposterous inefficiency. Try buying a plane ticket over the phone. Chances are that, due to the rampant outsourcing that is going on, you'll be connected to someone in India or South-East Asia—and if you're as unlucky as I was, their command of the English language will leave something to be desired. It must have taken me half an hour to book three tickets to Budapest. I had to spell every single word, and listen to him repeat it back to me. 'F for Foxtrot, O for Oscar…' It wasn't good enough to say 'Wing…like a plane has'. No, we had to go through the whole routine: 'W for Waste of Time, I for Imbecile, N for No Fucking Idea...' As Turkish will testify, I was drained by the time I finally got off the phone, but I was consoled by the fact that the ordeal was at least over. Wrong! A week later, my ticket arrived under the name of 'Glenn Sowler'. Silly me—I should have realised he said 'Soxtrot'. If your ticket name doesn't match your passport name, you don't fly. So, it was back on the phone for Round Two.

One day I had the temerity to try to purchase a pair of shoes in Oxford Street, London's shopping Mecca—well, at least for the average Joe and Jill. (There are far posher places.) I'll never forget the indifference with which I was treated. Requiring some advice, I stood there limp for at least one full minute, a shoe in each hand, looking in the direction of four employees. I was thinking: 'How obvious is it that I want help?' I'm sure they were thinking: 'Gee, I wish I could get this annoying bit of chicken out from between my teeth' or 'I'll be finished in four hours and then I can go home and watch *Eastenders*'. It was so laughable that I began to laugh. This finally attracted their attention and I received the bare minimum of assistance. I left without making a purchase and they couldn't have cared less. I'm accustomed to getting too much help in shops, and it pains me to constantly say: 'Just looking, thanks'. I didn't realise how good I had it until I went to the UK.

At this point, I'd like to be able to tell you the details of several run-ins I had at banks. Alas, I cannot. They have been permanently erased from my memory.

The preceding anecdotes surely beg the question: 'Why don't they do things differently?' In my quest to have bank clerks, estate agents, council workers and salespeople lift their respective games, I received the answer to this question numerous times: 'It's always been done like this'. Not: 'You're right, perhaps it would make more sense to do it that way' or 'I'll mention it to my boss'. No, if there wasn't a precedent, they weren't interested.

This told me something about the British—they are stuck in their ways. An American guy I met, totally unprompted, described it to me one day. He suggested that the Brits are 'mentally constipated'—in other words, they need a jolly good unblocking before they can progress. This is precisely the description for which I had been looking.

2. The British are affected by the weather.

Respectable medical journals like *The Lancet* have published studies on Seasonal Affective Disorder (SAD). Researchers seem to agree that one's level of happiness and emotional wellbeing is directly proportionate to the amount of sunlight to which one is exposed (or, some suggest, the amount of sunlight one receives on the backs of one's knees). Sounds a little bizarre, doesn't it? Bear with me whilst I think this through. If the theory were true, that would make people in tropical countries—or those closest to the equator—the happiest people on Earth. Could this be true? Are Queenslanders happier than Tasmanians? And what if they wear trousers?

I've been tossing around an idea in my head lately that the most powerful empires throughout history have tended to come from colder climes. The Aztecs and the Mayas, and perhaps more significantly the Egyptians, buck this trend somewhat, but I'm wondering if there's something to it. Maybe it's just that the people in hot areas have always been too relaxed or too content—or just too bloody happy—to bother with world domination. Perhaps they decided that their tropical paradise was quite enough, thank you very much. Those who elected the site of Canberra as Australia's seat of national government acknowledged this concept to a degree. The area was chosen partly for its 'bracing climate'—I guess they thought people would have no reason to leave the office and would therefore get on with running the country.

Anyway, I can tell you from experience that the Poms aren't getting much sunlight on the backs of their knees. There's more to it than their considerable distance from the equator. The British Isles are positioned on the Atlantic fringe, and hence cop every storm, squall and gale in that region. Turkish, being a science teacher, tells me that when cold air from the North Atlantic meets warm air from the south, this causes some sort of spinning phenomenon and, as a result, it 'pisses down'—right over Britain. Anyone who has been there for any length of time will know that the weather in Britain is predominantly shithouse. Winter drags on for about eight months, and you really only get a couple of weeks of summer. You should see the Poms on a genuinely warm, sunny day: construction workers get their shirts off, people leave work early to sit in beer gardens, and everybody's mood lifts appreciably.[17] Days like this, though, are few and far between.

I'm convinced that the stultifying monotony of Britain's poor weather impacts upon the moods and personalities of its inhabitants. I have heard people refer to the Brits as 'a depressed race'. I wouldn't go that far, but even the most upbeat of them seem to carry the scars of people who have lived through lots and lots (and lots) of really bleak days.

3. The British are not good with distances.

After my mum returned from spending a few weeks in Liverpool in 1993, she told us that quite a few of the people she had met (most middle-aged and older) had never been outside of the UK. This amazed me then and, come to think of it, I'm still amazed now. Surely, one of Britain's distinct advantages (for opportunists like me at least) is its proximity to Europe—the ultimate playground for tourists. More than forty countries, each comprising a

---

[17] When they're backpacking in Australia, they seem to be 'high on life' the entire time. I guess it helps that they are getting close to three Aussie dollars for every pound.

myriad of different cultural and linguistic experiences, are within several hours travel time. (And that's not counting North Africa, which is also pretty close.) It strikes me that things are changing, and that Poms are getting into the travel thing. Quite a few of my British friends had been abroad, though they were generally the open-minded ones—otherwise I wouldn't have been their friend. When I was trekking in the Andes in 2000, I met a heap of Poms. And they love coming to Australia. Just go to Manly in Sydney and you'll work that out. Once I went to a Coldplay concert in Sydney and, due to a survey conducted by the lead singer, I learned that more than half of the audience were British. Having said all this, I still think there are a lot of Pommies—of all ages— who have made little effort to see anything outside of their own backyard. Some may have fried themselves for ten days on a Mediterranean party island—others haven't even done that.[18] Perhaps it comes from an old 'cultural superiority' thing. You know: 'What could the Froggies or the Iti's possibly do better than us?' But I suspect a lot of it comes from a (to an Australian) warped perspective of distance. When distances are small, it seems, slightly greater distances seem *a lot* greater.

Australia is a bloody big place. Hence, I regard the distance from Canberra to Sydney as a short one. Several times, I have made this three and half hour trip for the sole purpose of going to a party, before returning in the morning. I've even gone up and back on weeknights to see concerts by international artists. I suspect most Brits would think I was nuts for doing this, and here's my anecdotal evidence for saying so.

Soon after we bullied our way into our rental accommodation in Hitchin, Grace, Kevin and I began the task of obtaining

---

[18] I do acknowledge that there are probably quite a few Aussies who have had their travel experiences limited to their home state and possibly Bali. To be fair, some states are extremely large. But I guess it's all relative.

furniture, whitegoods and the like. Kev and I spent one very busy night driving around Hertfordshire, purchasing items that we had seen advertised in various local rags. As it turns out, we got lucky with everything except a washing machine. The next day we saw a reasonably priced one advertised and, as we had been forced to return our hire van, the fact that they were offering to deliver it was an attraction. Given that the town they were in was fifteen miles away, I thought we were set.

'Oh no,' said the lady on the phone. 'If you're way down in Hitchin, we couldn't possibly do that. That's fifteen miles. Sorry love.' It took me a couple of hours to come to terms with the fact that they were prepared to lose a sale for the sake of a fifteen-minute drive. When I noticed that that particular washing machine was still being advertised a fortnight later, I recommenced banging my head against my living room wall. Still, if we had bought that one, we wouldn't have bought the one we eventually did buy. And if we hadn't bought that one, we wouldn't have met the two blokes who came around to install it for us. And then I wouldn't have witnessed a priceless scene in which Grace was standing nervously in the kitchen corner (her relief obvious when I walked in) while two long-haired, smelly pot-smokers drunkenly installed the machine, in between asking Grace if she was 'goin' out tonight'. It was a lot funnier once they'd left. One of them was absolutely off his dial!

Some quite close friends didn't make it to my thirtieth, citing travel problems. Although I've considered the idea that they were making an excuse in order to avoid watching me make a drunken ass of myself, or that they in fact secretly hated my guts, I'm inclined to believe their stated reason. I think twenty or thirty miles was just too far to drive. On the other hand, Juan, the Australian guy I had met in Spain, travelled two and a half hours by several trains to get there. I don't know if I can recall getting such a boost at a social event. Cheers Juan.

4. The British have highly questionable diets.

Although Britain has numerous high profile TV chefs, all of whom no doubt produce amazing things, I'm not sure who's actually eating these culinary delights. My experience with the Poms is: If it doesn't come with chips or bacon, it's not real food.

Bacon and chips, burger and chips, steak and chips, egg and chips, I can understand—in small doses. When it comes to curry and chips, though, I draw the line. Indian and Chinese takeaway owners (the latter universally, and somewhat politically incorrectly, referred to as 'Chinkies') quickly cottoned on to the British obsession with the humble chip. As accompaniment to each of their dishes, one is usually expected to choose between rice and chips. In many Asian restaurants and takeaways, in fact, you can choose to forget the Asian cuisine altogether. They will offer several British dishes, like steak and chips or half-chicken and chips. Most patrons, I'm sure, ignore these farcical options and embrace Asian dishes. Many Brits will tell you that their national dish is in fact a 'curry and a pint'—especially if the curry comes with chips!

I can almost understand the British attachment to the chip—there isn't much else they can call their own. (Even chips are French, aren't they?) The Scottish haggis is quite nice actually, if you like a rich, meaty taste (and once you get over the fact that it's actually sheep's bits cooked in a sheep's gut), but food connoisseurs worldwide are hardly filling their shopping baskets with the stuff. There is the dessert 'spotted dick' of course, though I think they only sell those to people like me, who get a giggle out of putting on a European accent and saying to the waiter: 'I have a spotted dick.' Then there's the pasty. I'm sure I'm missing others, but the point needs to be made. When one goes out to dinner, it is generally for some Italian, some Japanese, some Thai—I can't ever remember saying: 'I've got a real craving for some British!' Now I know that, traditionally, Australia doesn't have much to boast about in this regard. Take out novelties like pavlova and the lamington, and we've generally relied heavily upon the ideas of our non-British immigrants. But we've only had a couple of hundred years to be creative—not a couple of thousand!

I'll conclude this section with a cry for help. Can somebody please explain to me why so many British girls combine a discussion about how fat they are (whether this is true or grossly exaggerated is neither here nor there) with a hearty meal of a bacon burger and chips? My theory is that many are woefully uneducated on nutrition. Others, I suspect, know it's bad but can't escape from the cycle of eating what they perceive as *normal* dinner food. Or is this craving for fatty, starchy food, as some scientists suggest, just another symptom of SAD?

5. The British are crap at sport and care too much about football (soccer).

I lumped these two points together because I suspect that they might be related. Let me explain.

Apart from a few rowers, some jockeys, a couple of golfers and the superb distance runner Paula Radcliffe, the Poms are struggling at sport. In fact, the British Government responded to Britain's dismal medal tally at the 1996 Atlanta Olympic Games by conducting a national inquiry. What I'm not going to do at this point is list the sports (most notably team sports) in which Australia thrashes England. It has been very well-documented, to the point where British people have started to think of Australians as a race of people who try to make up for an inferiority complex by succeeding at sport. Yes, I know—it's just sour grapes. The fact that we constantly beat them doesn't make us feel superior—it's just funny how it *always* happens! Well, almost always. When I was in England, the Poms beat Australia in the first rugby league Test. What a lot of Australians probably don't realise, and what the British will tell you with pride, is that rugby league is only really played in two northern counties—Yorkshire and Lancashire. In short, hardly anybody cares about the sport. One never even hears about it outside of those parts. But boy, did I hear about it that week! And they reckon we've got inferiority complexes. Luckily, Australia won the final two tests convincingly, and the rot was stopped.

Around the same time, an Australian was crowned world champion at darts. The irony was not lost on the Poms. Here is a sport where you become good by hanging around in pubs all day, drinking beer, smoking cigarettes and eating pork pies (with chips)—a sport that is custom-made for the British—and now Australians are beating them at that too! I wished I could have been over there when we beat them at football (soccer—I know, it's a pain to keep having to write that). This had been the last bastion of British sporting supremacy and, although it was a 'friendly', they got done 3–1. The feeling was summed up by 1 email that was circulated. It was a photograph of an Australian fan at the game holding a sign: 'If we win, you suck at everything.'

Now we shouldn't kid ourselves—England has a better soccer team than Australia. Frankly, they'd bloody well want to. I contend that the attention the sport receives in Britain is downright unhealthy. I've already told you how consumed my students were by football, and it's not just the youth. It dominates the lives of Poms of all ages to an extent that we cannot comprehend. The closest thing Australia has to this is the passion of Melburnians for Australian Rules, but I'm convinced it doesn't equate. I was once in a British pub where, despite threats of ejection, a patron stood at the bar during a televised game grumbling, 'I fucking haaaate Beckham'. And he really meant it. There are all sorts of rivalries generated by football, and some of them are incredibly bitter. When Sol Campbell transferred from Tottenham Hotspur to rival club Arsenal, security guards had their work cut out to stop people, armed with signs bearing the terms 'Traitor' and 'Judas', ripping his head off as he entered the ground. I know for a fact that that level of intensity does not exist in Australian sport. Maybe it's not simply a British thing though—

maybe it's a football thing. Hooliganism (which, admittedly, is not always purely about football) exists on the continent too.

The point I'm trying to make here is that, when it comes to sport, England seems to put all its eggs into one basket. All sports are marginalised to accommodate the football obsession. In the sports sections of newspapers, football fills at least the first sixteen pages. Ludicrously, this is pretty much the case even during the off-season, when rumours of various transfers take pride of place.[19] It's enough to make one almost feel sorry for the English cricketers. Not only do they get thumped on the field—they're relegated to page seventeen of the sports pages.

Nevertheless, this state of affairs doesn't stop a great many English gentlemen regularly turning out in their whites for an afternoon on the cricket field. In my final week in England, my mate Ed invited me to participate in a cricket match. I really enjoyed the smell of freshly cut grass, and the sound of wood on leather (occasionally—they were Poms after all). It was a thoroughly relaxing afternoon. I must say, though, that all of the players, regardless of their level, seemed to be taking things rather seriously. It was a game between a law firm and the employees of one of their major clients. I guess these *are* the sorts of people who do tend to take things rather seriously. As a ring-in, I was excluded from the batting line-up but got to run around in the field. Taking two catches in the covers (one a sharp chance) was enough to earn me a bowl. I bowled a bloke on my second delivery, before having two 'sitters' dropped by one apologetic, uncoordinated chap. 'Good show,' they said to me after the game. 'How much cricket have you played?' 'I played once in primary school,' I replied. (You needn't have played

[19] I know it's not just the English who are obsessed with football. In fact, soccer dominates the sporting landscape of many countries. And don't get me wrong; I do enjoy English football and I do miss being there to cheer Arsenal on. I just think it's important to remember that, in sport as in everything else (except women, darling), variety is the spice of life.

competition cricket to know what to do—everyone grew up playing backyard cricket, didn't they?) 'Bloody Australians!' they said. 'They're good at everything!' I didn't argue.

6. The British really don't like redheads.

A strange one to round out the half-dozen I know, but it's one that really struck me.

My thoughts on redheads, prior to living in the UK, were these:
- Some people have red hair.
- I'm kind of glad I don't.
- It looks great on some women.
- If a bloke has it, you call him 'Bluey' (ironic), 'Blood Nut' (crude) or 'Chutney Crotch' (even cruder).
- All redheaded Australian Rules footballers play for Geelong.

In other words, no big deal.

The Poms, I was soon to find out, have a real problem with redheads. They call them 'Gingers', poke all sorts of fun at them, and occasionally ostracise them. It's quite weird. If you have red hair, forget trying to win an argument, 'cause when an insulting remark is topped off with 'Ginge', it's good night buddy. I know this because I saw it happen in the schoolyard, in the staffroom, on the sports field and on the street. And I saw many a redhead take it on the chin and ruefully accept their lowly place on the social ladder. I want a study done. I'd like to know how many British emigrants are redheads. Lots, I reckon. Maybe the Geelong scout waits at the airport.

As I approach the end of this chapter, I wonder if I've been able to capture something of the British mindset. They're not a bad lot. They just have strange ideas about a few things—ideas that take a bit of getting used to if you come from a place 20 000 kilometres away. Still, when one considers how far apart our two countries are, our people are pretty similar (exception: Slothwick). I estimate that we're about eighty-one per cent socially compatible.

I've made a lot of generalisations in this chapter. I cannot make a generalisation about the anecdote I'm about to relate, but I find myself unable to leave it out.

One of the most disturbing things I saw in Britain was on the regional TV news one evening. The lead story—yes, the lead story—involved a visit by the Queen and the then-alive Queen Mother to a local fair to judge a coat-hanger decorating competition. To think that some people in Australia actually voted *for* a republic![20] Do they not recognise true leadership when they see it?

One more thing: Should you go to the UK at any point, following the rules below will save you ridicule and embarrassment. Be thankful, because I found out the hard way.

1. Say 'trousers', not 'pants'. Pants are underpants. Boy, did I regret it the day I demanded (in accordance with school rules) that the scruffy lads in my class tuck their shirts into their pants.
2. Say 'vest', not 'tank top' or 'singlet'. I know it makes no sense, a vest being an overgarment, not an undergarment. Just do it.
3. Say 'break', not 'recess'. (For teachers only, really.) If you say recess, they will really have no idea what you're talking about.
4. Say 'football', not 'soccer'. Despite the fact that London is home to a well-known store called Soccer Scene; this term is seen as American and therefore unacceptable when referring to their game.
5. Do not say 'dollar' (as in 'I wish I had a dollar for every time…') or 'buck'. If they're anything like my ratbag students, they will laugh in your face.

Other than that, just keep your head down, buy a warm jacket, eat your chips, shout at the football on the TV, dye your hair if it's red, and you'll be okay. You might even enjoy yourself as much as I did in Old Blighty.

[20] Believe me, this is something for which the British really do, understandably, take the piss out of Australians.

Epilogue

As I write this in 2003, I am rapidly approaching the age of thirty-one. I am still several hundred dollars away from paying off the debt I incurred whilst travelling the world. I am engaged to be married, yet I cannot afford a ring, and the wedding itself is a looming financial hurdle. With property prices as they are, putting down a deposit on a first house seems like a pipe dream. Hell, I'm still chipping away at my HECS[21] debt, more than eight years after I completed my university studies.

To my name, I have a car and personal effects. My teacher's salary is reasonable...I suppose. A\$45,000 per year for a five year trained honours graduate with eight years working experience would be laughable in certain professions, but it could be worse— I could be a nurse.

Many my age have made the choice to work hard (in a well-paying profession), to settle down, put a few pennies away, buy property (at a time when prices were within reason), and make significant progress along the road to financial security and even a degree of affluence. Every now and again, just for a moment, I envy them. Life, though, is all about choices, and I made a different one.

In the last six years, I have been overseas on six different occasions. I have visited thirty-two countries across six continents. I have been to the summit of great mountains and to the centre of lifeless deserts. I have sweltered in the heat of the tropics, basked in the glorious sunshine of temperate regions, and frozen my tits off above the Arctic Circle. I have bunked down in palaces, in private homes and in tiny huts. I have spent time with people from numerous ethnic, cultural, religious, social and economic

---

[21] Higher Education Contribution Scheme, an Australian government loan scheme for university courses...or a tax for tertiary students.

backgrounds. I have regularly left my comfort zone. I have met funny, interesting, friendly, compassionate, beautiful people. I have met rude bastards, small-time con men, pimps and drug dealers. I have learned about people and their histories. I have been able to draw parallels between events and personalities in the formation of various nations, and have reached a greater understanding of the human race and the commonality of our interests. I have seen how the other half live—in poverty, in squalor and in ignorance. I have questioned the status quo privately and publicly. I have admired and despaired at the way things are done. I have reached the heights of optimism and the depths of pessimism about our planet and those who inhabit it. I have thanked my lucky stars that I was born where I was, and that I was able to approach my independent life with a running start. I have envied those who have carved out their own little niche in the world and have found contentment and inner peace. I have taken time to smell the roses. My experiences have been, in turn, enlightening, uplifting and character building.

It might seem a lot to shell out A$50,000 for these experiences. I'd be sitting pretty now if I hadn't done it. But I'd be a far less knowledgeable, less tolerant and less interesting person. I am proud of the extra dimension that travel has given me. If I had my time again, I'd do exactly the same thing. I realise that things will settle down for me now…at least until the next time the travel bug bites.